108 Sonnets for Awakening

and Selected Poems

108 Sonnets
for Awakening

and Selected Poems

Alan Jacobs

BOOKS

Winchester, UK
Washington, USA

First published by O-Books, 2012
O-Books is an imprint of John Hunt Publishing Ltd., Laurel House, Station Approach,
Alresford, Hants, SO24 9JH, UK
office1@o-books.net
www.o-books.com

For distributor details and how to order please visit the 'Ordering' section on our website.

Text copyright: Alan Jacobs 2011

ISBN: 978 1 84694 947 0

A CIP catalogue record for this book is available from the British Library.

Design: Stuart Davies

Printed in the USA by Edwards Brothers Malloy

We operate a distinctive and ethical publishing philosophy in all
areas of our business, from our global network of authors to
production and worldwide distribution.

CONTENTS

SELECTED POEMS

To My beloved Sat-Guru Sri Bhagavan Ramana Maharshi whose lotus feet graciously touched my soul and is saving me from drowning in the dread sea of samsara.

FOREWORD

108 SONNETS FOR AWAKENING is a Sonnet Sequence along with some Selected Poems that has been composed primarily for those interested in Self Realisation and the Non Dual Philosophy of Advaita Vedanta . They are also written for all who enjoy this beautiful well tried and tested poetic form, which so powerfully drives a single point home with remarkable precision. As there are several Sanskrit or Tamil words in the text, I have appended a brief glossary of words used. 108 is regarded as an auspicious number that is often used to numerate the stanzas in sacred Sanskrit and Tamil Poetry.

Alan Jacobs
President
Ramana Maharshi Foundation UK
London and Tiruvannamalai
July 2011

PREAMBLE

SCORN NOT THE SONNET

Scorn not the Sonnet; Critic, you have frowned,
Mindless of its just honours; with this key
Shakespeare unlocked his heart; the melody
Of this small lute gave ease to Petrarch's wound;
A thousand times this pipe did Tasso sound;
With it Camoens soothed an exile's grief;
The Sonnet glittered a gay myrtle leaf
Amid the cypress with which Dante crowned
His visionary brow: a glow-worm lamp,
It cheered mild Spenser, called from Faery-land
To struggle through dark ways; and when a damp
Fell round the path of Milton, in his hand
The Thing became a trumpet; whence he blew
Soul-animating strains—alas, too few!

William Wordsworth

1

ALL BEINGS YEARN TO BE HAPPY

A SONNET CORONA

All beings yearn to be happy, always;
Happiness without a tinge of sorrow,
To enjoy a life of carefree days,
Taking no burden of thought for tomorrow.
When restless mind's at peace in deep sleep,
What glimpse of worry, grief or despair?
So happiness lies within, buried down deep.
How to find this treasure, awake, aware?
Ask the question, who am I, and from where?
That's the essential means of the holy task,
Ending ego's 'me' and 'my', that's there.
No pleasure endures in things of this Earth,
Enquire within, who basks behind our mask?
To regain that Selfhood we lost at birth.

2

TO REGAIN THAT SELFHOOD

To regain that Selfhood we lost at birth,
First consider well the cinema screen,
To understand that, gains merit and worth.
On the screen there appears a tense drama,
The film begins and we enjoy the show.
Fire, flood, sex, death, a vast panorama;
The screen's unchanging, but the film's a shadow.
The simile teaches, strange as it may be,
That both seer and seen make up the mind.
On Consciousness as screen, all action's based.
To know that is true, is the clue to be free,
A guiding beacon that's so rare to find,
Now and forever for eternity,
That's the Sage wisdom by which we are graced.

3

SAGE WISDOM

That's the Sage wisdom by which we are graced,
We're taught the silver screen as a metaphor.
Seated in theatre stalls, now we are placed,
To proceed with clarity and enquire some more.
The bright theatre lamp is the light supreme,
Illuminating both actors and the scene.
We see stage and the play only by light,
Yet when action ends, the lamp remains bright.
Just as woven cloth and its colour white
Are never, ever perceived as apart,
So when mind and light both unite,
They form ego, knotted and bound in the heart.
Of all that we've ever learned since birth,
That's the high wisdom proclaimed on Earth.

4

HIGH WISDOM

That's the high wisdom proclaimed on Earth,
How to make mind to merge in its source?
Only by enquiring with all of one's force,
The central question regarding its birth,
The ultimate scrutiny of "Who Am I"?
As thoughts froth forth like waves on the ocean,
They'll all be slain by such introspection,
Unveiling the Self, the lost inward eye.
Pearls lay buried on the deep ocean floor,
Attracting divers to search for this goal.
Holding their breath they plunge to the core
Of the ocean bed, for the pearl oyster's soul.
To gain this gem in the heart's sacred place,
Just seek for the source where mind is based.

5

SEEK FOR THE SOURCE

Just seek for the source where mind is based.
You travel alone on a mystery train;
By this metaphor we're comfortably placed,
To travel by providence free from pain.
So put all your heavy luggage on the rack,
Only a fool carries it on his head!
Be glad, accept the predestined track,
Rest quietly, safe at home on your bed!
Surrender in joyful jubilation!
Surrender utterly to God's almighty will,
Surrender with total resignation,
Surrender knowing all will be well,
Surrender whole heartedly with one accord,
Take safe refuge in the all loving Lord!

6

TAKE SAFE REFUGE

Take safe refuge in the all loving Lord!
For life's a dream and sleeping dreams are short,
The waking dream is long; both stem from thought.
The Real is beyond both this waking and sleep.
The sword of enquiry slays dream states deep,
So reaching their substratum, numinous,
The state of pure consciousness, Self luminous!
Blissfully aware, yet awake in sleep.
As the cockerel crows ready to sup,
At the roseate dawn of first morning light,
Awareness pours into the near empty cup,
Granting a moment's taste of Self insight.
This light is the eye that forever sees,
Who can be known by enquiring "who frees?"

7

WHO CAN BE KNOWN BY ENQUIRY

Who can be known by enquiring "who frees?"
The Master who lives in the cave of the heart,
Not separate from one's Self, being the start,
Of the final search from bond to release.
The Sage appears when the soul is ready,
With strong gaze of grace he says "be aware
That God and his wisdom are already there!"
He acts as a brake to make the mind steady,
While mercy flows freely in sunshine and air,
Hindered only by our being unready.
If you come to him, meekly with an empty cup,
His grace is then bound to fill it up.
The Master's glance is the grace of the Lord,
He cuts you free with his mighty sword.

8

HE CUTS YOU FREE

He cuts you free with his mighty sword,
To guide you surely, on the upward way
To Self Realisation, your real birthday!
Consummation of "That" the Sage's word,
Is "rest in the Self," which is always heard.
In him, place great trust and affirm, say yea
As certainty! Our Real Self blazes away,
Ever surrendered to the almighty Lord,
Revealing great peace for Realisation's sake,
Renouncing belief that a rope is a snake.
The seeker surely becomes "the great find",
His own blissful being, the summit in kind,
This great Teaching eternally frees,
One with the Self, as the Absolute sees.

9

ONE WITH THE SELF

One with the Self, as the Absolute sees,
He answers all our prayers and our pleas;
We must first enter that dear sacred part,
Not the fleshy pump that throbs on the left,
But the sacred core: by being skilful and deft,
We find that on the right; is the real Heart!
By harnessing breath, being adept and bright,
We dive with great skill and all of our might,.
There dwelling in depths of our true Heart's cave,
Lives the shining "Unity" blazing as Self,
Pulsation of I-I, where all shadows cease.
So fixing gaze there, finally, off we stave,
Perverted, wandering, demonic mind elf,
Returning to "Self", our birthright of peace.

10

RETURNING TO SELF

Returning to Self, our birthright of peace,
Is knowing that all this vile body performs
Was predestined before it ever took form.
So from stress, despair and fretting, pray cease!
Our freedom dwells in our natural State,
Renouncing "I Am The Doer" notion,
Detached from fruit of form's puppet motion,
Yet grace can avert even predestined fate!
Be like a skilled actor on this stage of strife!
Play with goodwill the part you've been given,
No matter how strangely you find you are driven,
Knowing who, truly you are, in this life.
Until fate pulls down the final curtain,
Know you're Self not body, know that is certain!

11

KNOW YOU'RE THE SELF

Know you're Self not body, know that is certain!
In this Realisation, there's no cause to leave home,
You can strive in the city, there's no need to roam.
To change style of life would all be in vain,
For mind remains with you, until it is slain.
Demonic ghost ego, source and fabric of thought,
Create body and world, whereby we are caught.
Change of place, never changed the way we behave,
Whether living at home, in a forest or cave.
There are two ways by which our bonds may be freed:
Either ask "to whom is this strange fate decreed?"
Or surrender false 'me' to be then stricken down,
So praying intensely for 'my will' to cease,
We leave it to grace, to grant us release.

12

WE LEAVE IT TO GRACE

We leave it to grace, to grant us release.
God will do this through the gaze of his Sage,
He sends down His messenger for every age,
To those who yearn and pray for great peace.
The Realised Sage lives on here and now,
Without confusing the Self with the mind.
Humble, compassionate, loving and kind,
Wisely profound, as his way clearly shows.
He steers the vessel of firm devotees,
Fulfilling everyone's spiritual need.
In deep silence, he sits, with perfect ease,
To awaken those, whom his teaching well heed.
Graciously, his great glance of initiation,
Drives the mind inwards, to Self Realisation!

13

DRIVE THE MIND INWARDS

Driving the mind inwards, to Self Realisation,
He grants safe passage through life's stormy ocean;
What frail soul will ever be excluded
From the presence of the holy Supreme?
No matter how depraved or deluded,
His mercy never ends, and will always redeem,
Raising the soul from the depth of depression,
To free one from the 'I am this body' obsession.
From passions that churn desire and aversion,
His fair breeze wafts clear equanimity;
Enmeshed no more in worldly adversity,
Never perturbed by praise nor foul enmity,
We learn that there's the greatest giving
In knowing all are Self, and so truly living.

14

KNOW ALL ARE THE SELF

In knowing all are Self, and so truly living,
We thank the great Sage who is ever giving.
We praise the Lord, who leads us to his feet,
His gracious gaze is eternally sweet,
Without ceasing, he's forever reviving,
He grants that freedom, our real surviving.
He severs the grip of bondage's chains,
He frees the soul, where confusion reigns,
He bestows both compassion and deep peace,
He sends out his grace to grant us release.
He teaches the truth that Consciousness is all,
And Self Enquiry to raise us up from our fall.
We praise God Almighty whom is ever living,
This crown of my verses is our thanksgiving!

15

REGAIN THAT SELFHOOD

To regain that Selfhood we lost from birth,
That's the Sage wisdom by which we are graced,
This is the high wisdom proclaimed on Earth.
Just seek for the source where mind is based.
Take refuge in the all loving Lord,
Who can be known by enquiring 'who frees?'
He cuts you loose with his mighty sword,
One with the Self, as the Absolute sees.
Returning to Self, our birthright of peace,
Know you're Self, not body, know that is certain!
We leave it to grace, to grant us release.
He drives the mind inwards, to Self Realisation,
In knowing all are Self, and so truly living,
This Sonnet Corona is my thanksgiving!

16

MOUNTAIN SONG

Ravens love ravening among ripening redish grapes so fine,
But beware of little foxes or there'll be no foaming wine
Of ecstasy this morn, ushered in by radiant ruby dawn,
When prayer and meditation declare one's soul's to be reborn.

Striding up the sacred roseate mountain path, laughing loud,
Far away from the noisy, hurried, bustling maddening crowd,
While lucid dew drops, rainbow edged, grace the heavenly
scene,
Pilgrim laughs, striving hard to wake up from his daunting
dream
Of worldly life, which prisons sleeping mankind's restless
throng.
So now he fills his lungs with air and sings a joyful song.

"Trust that great magnificent power which truly knows the way,
It thrives inside our own dear Self. If we honour 'That' each day,
All will be well, very, very well, unfolding as it should,
Then be free, from dream world's threatening throttling wood!

17

EGOECHTEMY

The laser beam of finely tuned attention
Dives inwards with breath and thought retention,
Searching for the source of 'phantom me'
It cuts though all the sheaths and veils we see,
Of habits, thought forms and selfish will,
Formed over daring dream affairs often ill.
The Pearl Diver finds nothing on the floor
Of this deep interior ocean bed; what's more,
One day his head falls right into his Heart,
He sees the ego source and watches it depart.
Boom! Boom, it shakes and flies right out the door.
The binding knot's been severed and for ever more.
Successful open heart surgery, has been performed
Liberation! Poor suffering soul's no more deformed.

18

THE ARCH USURPER

To claim I am the sole doer all alone,
Is the cardinal crime of woman and man;
It means that ego's usurped God's throne.
To be free of this grave sin, if we can,
Surrender monkey mind at His lotus feet,
Then Self Enquire with all of one's might.
This way we'll soon be whole and complete,
Revealing Self, source of truth and light.

The Universe rests in God Almighty's arms,
In joy of pure existence, reality, bliss,
Aspirants are blest by heavenly charms,
Inside our heart we receive God's kind kiss.
Let Him take over the heavy burden of our life,
To end all restless mental storm and endless strife.

19

AUGUST ROSES

I saw the lustre of a radiant dawn,
Reflected in an august summer rose;
Gold, yellow, orange, ravishing red,
Blended to form the blazing flame of morn.
I held the fiery flower up to my nose,
To sense the fragrance of her perfumed head,
Bewitched by all the colours of that form.

Then I deeply turned my gaze inside,
To see what dwelt there, in my inner soul;
What impression had this rose made on me?
I waited some while, at heart I did abide.
That rose was a pointer to make me whole,
Reflecting that great dawn when I'd be free
And ego, in penitential fire, had truly died.

20

AUBURN AUTUMN

An awesome auburn dawn stripes billowing clouds,
Pebbling, pie balding them in piece meal array,
As grace removes our puzzled mind's grey shrouds,
We're set to welcome yet one more auspicious day.
Are we like the Egyptian scarab beetle's state,
Shovelling our dung before us until wings sprout,
And we learn to fly away to freedom, and await
A transformed life, in purer peaceful calm no doubt?

Autumn comes and auburn leaves fall from weeping trees,
According to God's predestined heavenly will;
Their radiant tones remind us that we please
Him most, when we engage enquiry, up to our fill.
Fiery red and gold, flare autumn's burnished tones,
Our scarab shell falls dead, our soul now speeds back home!

21

PROTECT AND GUARD

Oh Shiva, purest one, may Brahma live long!
Protect and guard his remaining four heads,
He's ordained the poverty to which I'm led
In this false dream world of right and wrong.
What fear is left for me when I sing this song
And Thy gaze of love, to me has said,
"Have faith, in me , my child, you do belong,
I will save you from the spiritually dead."

A son is lost and from home does stray,
His father looks for him everywhere,
Then on one marvellous miraculous day,
He's found and delivered safely there,
Back to his land at blissful peace at last,
Clasped in Lord Shiva's arms, tight and fast.

22

FORGET-ME-NOT

Pretty petulant petals of brightest blue,
Petty adornment gracing gardens of love,
Emblem of Adoration to our Great Lord above,
For Remembering Him is right worship true;
Prayer will bring God ever closer to you,
As Noah knew, when he saw a snow white dove,
That showed the end of that flood, which drove
Righteousness from Earth, except for a chosen few.

When man falls into a dark ditch too low,
God in his mercy sends His messenger down,
To lift up the level in both country and town.
Thus we'll never forget Him, and even more so
Remain loyal as His flock, in order to know
Salvation, when we gain Enlightenment's crown.

23

SUN FLOWER

Radiant floral emblem of my Real Self,
Hiding behind her veil. Try then to find
Her, not mischievous monkey mind,
Nor dark demonic perverted elf,
Avaricious for his material pelf,
Egotistic and spiritually blind,
Ever spinning thoughts that weave and wind,
Piling up more baggage on his mental shelf.
The Great Sun in my Self is not like these,
But the Source of Conscious-Awareness-Light,
Dispersing dark gloom of sad ignorant night,
God-like, that immortal power which frees
Bound soul from its malevolent disease,
Bringing her back home to new heavenly height.

24

PINK LOTUS

Pink lotus, emblem of the Hindu wisdom sage,
Greatest aid to spiritual growth for man.
If one learns their teachings and carefully scan
The practise needed for this decadent age,
An inner struggle the aspirant must wage.
Pink lotus is rooted in muddy mire, but can
Still open as a bloom of beauty better than
Known by those who're blind to God's Almighty plan.

A soul lived a life of gross indulgence,
But tired of pleasure she turned to learn
Truth necessary for her repentance,
Self Realisation to surely earn.
Her ignorance and sin were fertile ground
To turn within. True wisdom she quickly found.

25

ROSE GARDEN

In my rose garden warmly rouged by dawn,
There grow white arum lilies shining too,
Prinked with iris, softly clad in blue.
Radiant roses glow crimson like the morn,
I stroll amongst the fountains in my view
Such Lady Beauty spoke as Being True.
True in the sense that Art is Beauty born,
To waken souls of men to our Great God divine,
And save him from a sorry fate, sad and forlorn.
That garden was the threshold to that place,
Enriched by brilliant bright sunshine.
I felt the gentle hand of blessed grace,
That rose garden was truly Highest Art,
A joy that moved me from the depth of heart.

26

DAFFODIL

Easter Lily, named by those whose blooms we love,
Golden yellow, surging wild in wood or field,
They open fresh perfumed petals to yield
To sunlight, shining down from high above.
We wait for the sign of that peaceful dove
To save us from Noah's flood when soul is healed,
And our covenant with God is truly sealed,
And demon ego receives his killing shove.

Emblem of all that's good in Christ's Teaching,
The Easter Lily shines as floral light,
The Christian Way of Love is ever reaching
The hearts of those who for redemption fight.
This flower of Beauty feeds the yearning soul,
Of those who crave salvation, and again made whole.

27

BLUEBELL WOOD

I took a walk in nearby Bluebell wood,
A wild flower garden arched by aspen trees,
When sunshine casts its searchlight beam on these,
We're raised to God, the blessed and the good.
This is the home of Beauty if it's understood;
Art without Her will always cease to please,
Nor take Soul back to worship on her knees,
As poetry, music, painting truly should.

A painter came to Bluebell Wood to catch
Its wonder on his canvas. In due course
Try as he might, his skill could never match
The magic marvel of Mother Nature's force.
He realised there was a limit to his power
To capture such God-like beauty in that sacred hour.

28

JOY RIDE

Joyful jubilation is the jester's song,
Sweet tonic to right all doleful wrong.
From the heart it rings a cheerful chime,
And rescues mind from dull depressive time.
So roar from the roof tops with all ones might,
God shines from His heaven and all is right!
Bury sad melancholy in a deep black hole,
And much sooner save poor suffering soul.

Laughter makes us loose all worry and care,
So unbutton one's coat and let down one's hair!
The world's not a place for shame or for woe,
That's a very quick route to hell as we know.
'Row, row, row, the boat gently down the stream,
Merrily, merrily for life is but a dream'!

THE GOLDEN ROAD TO SAMARKAND

PROEM

Sweet to ride forth at evening from the wells,
When shadows pass gigantic on the sand,
And softly through the silence beat the bells,
Along the Golden Road to Samarkand.

We travel not for trafficking alone;
By hotter winds our fiery hearts are fanned:
For love of knowing what should not be known,
We take the Golden Road to Samarkand.

James Elroy Flecker

29

THE CARAVAN OF DREAMS

We're carted in a cosy caravan of dreams,
Driving fast across vast desert waste.
Nothing we see is exactly as it seems,
From mirage to death we race in reckless haste.
The Master Sheikh cries "wake up you sleeping one,
Within you shines the Great Almighty Sun!".
A boy had cause to cross that golden sand,
To find his fond father in Samarkand.
His journey was beset by many trials,
The brave lad trekked for miles and miles.
He trudged on when all seemed sadly lost,
He persisted regardless of all human cost.
God's grace came in camel shape, a beast had strayed,
So back to his father, his way was safely made!

30

THE BLAZING DESERT

The fierce blazing heat of noon-day Sun,
Afflicts each caravan on its lonely way.
The camels yearn for water, but there is none,
Until they reach some oasis, one blessed day.
The Sheikh cries "The Sun is like God's will,
Driving your caravan across the golden sand;
Water's like Real Truth, which you need to fill
Your heart, and cut your knot of bondage band!"

A traveller traversed across that desert plane,
Soon he became thirsty from the blazing heat,
He prayed for water from a fall of rain,
To save his life, his journey then complete.
He glimpsed an oasis, 'twas a mirage it seems,
Such is our wasted life, a caravan of dreams!

31

COME TO MY TAVERN

The Sheikh calls "come to my tavern, pray drink
Sweet ecstatic ruby wine of love divine!
Enquire into who's that one who thinks?
Soon you'll find your inner Sun sublime,
That lights your mind with wandering dreams,
And makes you see a world that only seems
As Real, when its all a dire delusion;
That's the very root of mind's illusion!"

A pilgrim knocked hard at the tavern door,
Alas he found it locked and firmly closed.
No answer came, although he did implore
The Sheikh to help in all he had proposed.
Then he heard a voice within the tavern cry,
"My son to ego-mind, you first must die!"

32

THE ONE ETERNAL SHEIKH

The One Eternal Sheikh is our blessed Self,
Not treacherous, perverted monkey mind,
Like some diabolic demonic elf,
It flits from every tree to tree it finds.
So hearken to the wisdom of one's Master Sheikh,
As he teaches freedom, and the way to wake.
The Sheikh in the desert on the golden way
Frees us from the bleak jail of every day.

A man met his Master one blessed day,
And enquired, "how to free myself from 'mind'?"
The Master said "if you turn within my way,
In search of your own false self you'll surely find,
The real freedom you so urgently desire,
Be reborn again in God's sacramental fire!"

33

SONATA

Consciousness is like a clean sheet of paper,
A Sonnet from Real Heart is like a taper
Set to light that fire which burns all mental dross,
And frees sad clouded soul which needs that loss
Of dark ego, veiling her blazing sun of Self,
No longer loving worldly dreams and all the pelf
Of wealth, possession, jealousy and lust,
The clumsy clutter of mind's dirt and dust.

Now listen to the unstruck music start,
Heard in the cave of the spiritual heart,
Like a symphony of swift circling spheres,
Which cheer happy soul's sharp listening ears,
So she rejoices in Self, God and Life,
Full of gratitude, eternally free from strife!

34

FAITH

Take the deep leap into firm certainty of Faith
Let God's mighty mountain ranges be our shield
Against sense storms of restless monkey mind.Enjoy complete
untroubled care free unworried calm,
By handing over our whole bothersome burden
Of distress, concern, and imagined anxiety
About one's ordained duties and many affairs,
To our Lord of Love and infinite compassion,
Great Power in the heart, Self of our Being,
To whom we've unconditionally surrendered,
Taking sole refuge with worshipful devotion.
Even tribulation is welcomed as for the best!
We gain mind control through repetition of His Name,
And dive into the Heart, questing for the source of 'I',
Full of gratitude for his boundless love and grace.

35

EARNESTNESS

Life's not some glamorous gambling game,
A throw of mindless roulette on chances wheel.
We slipped from our Natural State the Self
And fell into some gross material dream,
Our angel wings were badly bruised and hurt.
After suffering we prayed to come back home,
And in Her Grace, Love sent our Unique Sage,
To wake us from our dark nightmarish plight;
Repeating birth and death through many lives,
Drowning in a whirlpool of ordained fate.

Surrender and Self Enquiry is the cure.
The Self which sent us on this ego trip
Aching, yearning, to find one's Self again
Will aid us, if strong earnestness sincere is sure..

36

ALMIGHTY POWER

Almighty Power shines bright from the light of Your lotus feet,
Our dearest Sat-Guru dwelling deep in the spiritual heart;
You nourish our souls with ambrosial nectar, honey sweet,
Ever gracious to aid our quest. Your sacred Jnana You impart
To those blessed devotees, earnest in their chosen sadhana.
We thank you for leading us to tread your holy mountain way,
We chant your praises daily oh Great Lord Bhagavan Ramana!
You makes life's dire dream well worth living every single day.

Your Almighty Power is brim filled with unconditional love,
You take us closer to our own True Self, a compassionate friend.
You've been sent to help us in our quest by Brahm who reigns
above,
You promise to ferry us to the other shore, right to life's end.
We wait to hear your inner voice in silence and solitude,
We attend your call,our hearts are filled with gratitude.

37

BRIDAL MARRIAGE

We delight in dawn's magenta red when we rise up,
From the black nightmare dream of sad samsara.
So raise on high the silver chalice wedding cup
To celebrate the advent of blest sat chit ananda!

Now the bridal marriage is consummated in bliss,
A thanksgiving to Sat-Guru dwelling in the heart,
Seal it with an everlasting devotional kiss,
To He who made miracles happen, from the start!
There's no real substance in life's dire dream,
All that appears on awareness' fine screen,
Is not dear friends what it appears to seem,
For Mother Maya deceives us in whatever's seen.
So pursue sadhana with all strength and fortitude,
And feel ones Great Power of love and gratitude!

38

SOUL'S GARDENER

The fertile soil of devotion must be tearfully tilled,
With persistent determined effort ones days be filled.

We remove all egotism's strangling climbing creeping weeds,
Then plant deeply and firmly, right intention's prayerful seeds.

The golden harvest rests in the palm of that Eternal One,
Whose mercy sends us refreshing grace of rain and wisdom's
Sun.

All overgrown shrubs of desire, we must carefully prune,
Or they'll deeply bury our well kept garden much too soon.

We water sweet roses and lilies with fond love and grace,
And make sure verge, edges and borders are well trimmed in
place.

All needs to be tenderly tended and well watched as it must,
Not abandoned by careless neglect and lack of great trust.

So once more we determine to make our fine garden whole,
And redeem this forsaken treasure for poor wandering Soul!

39

UNSTRUCK MUSIC

Tune in to the unstruck music of the heart,
Hear subtle ethereal sounds impart

Angelic melody from another place,
Where Souls at rest dwell in peace and grace.

It's the music of the heavenly spheres,
Only enjoyed by those who have the ears

To hear, as Lord Jesus once so wisely said,
'Pray begin to walk and take up your bed'.

This music is composed by rays of light,
Heard in the Self, but unseen by sight.

It's a magic mystery of sound profound,
Hear it once and demon ego is soon unbound.

So rejoice in this music to take one home,
It's all that's contained in the sound of OM!

40

ART OF INWARD TURNING

Like the dawn chorus of cheerful carolling birds,
Man's a restless creature made up of many words,
This mountain stream of thought is not blessing but a bane;
It clouds the Sun of Selfhood and leaves him sad in shame.

In order to climb up to a higher plane of Being,
We must cultivate the art of inward seeing;
With attention, yearn to find the source of I,
Which spills the verbal torrent made of 'me' and 'my'.

Questioning 'Who Am I' silences tyrant mind,
And instead of bubbling burble we soon will find
A flood of joy and bliss stemming from the heart,
Full of Grace and Love and ever ready to impart

Such is divine stillness and mystical power
Which the silent mind brings into perfect flower.

41

LOVELY LABURNUM

Lovely Laburnum emblem of golden rain,
A blessed shower of grace that's heaven sent
To each, when errant soul removes the stain
Of worldliness, now set on heaven bent
To search for the hidden source of I,
Buried deep in the Heart but quickly reached
Through Self Enquiry, seeking for the how and why
Egotism in its folly, true wisdom breached?
To end up in the waste land of sad samsara.

But thanks to the teaching of Great Lord Ramana,
We're freed from dread cycle of death and birth,
To be restored to Selfhood, our own true worth.
So when we admire the golden Laburnum tree,
We recall the loving grace that's sent by Thee!

42

CARAVANSARAI

We're trapped in a camel caravan moving to our certain death,
Wandering through a desert wasteland worn out and short of breath,
Doing our best but knowing we're not in any way the 'doers'
Anxious to avoid re-birth and be amongst the mournful losers.

But take great heart there's always the saving face of grace,
When divine compassion and mercy restores our original place,
To sheer existence, love, conscious awareness, reality, bliss,
When Self's at ease and peace and nothing more can ever go amiss!

When he treads on your errant soul with his sweet lotus feet.
You can rest assured you're in His tiger jaws and all's replete,
You can wholeheartedly surrender to His almighty will,
All shall proceed to Liberation nothing will ever go ill!

So we take care of our camel on its dry sandy desert march,
We water her with Truth so her tongue will never ever parch!

43

GRACE CONQUERS ALL

Problems can't be solved by poor puny thought;
Only the pure Grace of God can ever save.
Stupid mind will fail, but it's not mind's fault,
Brain's only doing what mind thinks it ought.

There's only One Doer, and to free he who's caught,
With his strong right hand He'll aid the brave,
And end the desires of all who senses crave,
Then struggle hard with ego and storm its fort.

Pilgrim climbing on the mountain path, one day
Realised that Self will help all those who persist,
By strong efforts, ever trying to resist
Demon prompting of ego mind, and persist.
Then God knows what to do, with all his might;
For the surrendered, freedom's well within their sight.

44

All ALONE

The wise Sage, unfathomable, free from fear,
In Heart's fair field, stands firm. His solitude
Fulfils the throbbing pulse of Earth's beatitude.
For those asleep, who time and space hold dear.
There's just One Existence for the Seer.
No place remains in his placid plenitude
For shadows 'real' or 'unreal' to occlude;
No more seems the Sun to rise or set, yet's here.

How, seeing golden Sun at play in our world,
Can he, whose natural state is Self empowered,
Perceiving a precious ring, see ought than gold?
As the lotus flowers, so is his life embowered.
Man awakened, remembers not his worldly dream,
His garb, the Self, is like a cloak without a seam.

45

COSMIC VISION

Imagine a tapestry of precious stones,
Diamond, topaz, ruby, tourmaline,
Sapphire, emerald, all cluster in between,
Ornamenting heaven with their rainbow tones.
Each reflected lustre each appears to own,
In harmony from galaxy to gene,
Inter-related, an ethereal scene
Enjoyed by Consciousness, One and all alone.
Uncaused, spontaneous, without an end,
Infinite jewels arise; gems of dust
Illuminated, mirroring as they must
The dance of cosmic music God did send.
All things dissolving to nothing at all
Rhythms of the spheres pulsate and fall.

46

ADAM'S DREAM

Poor modern Adam, so sadly forlorn,
The tread-mill of life has worn down his soul;
Sometimes he wished he'd never been born,
He yearns for a way to make himself whole.
Like a traveller lost in a bleak desert place,
Blinded by sense-storms with savour less food,
He begs for water, crying for grace,
He prays to discover the source of the Good.

Entrapped like a wasp on a jammed window pane,
He drones up and down, in search of the light,
Until falling exhausted, worn out by the strain,
He lies flat on his back, with no help in sight.
Through self surrender and intensive yearning
Answer comes from God's bright flame, ever burning.

47

A FATHER'S CALL

In Adam's slumbering mind arose a dream,
A warm compelling voice, a father's call,
Saying "don't weep!", and then a brighter gleam
Of light, unveils a scene which does enthral.
It was an orient land. On reddish earth,
The Sage sits smiling with firm and tender gaze,
Saying "I'll help you, dear child, find rebirth!"
His look is steady, his eyes are ablaze.

It was as if some summer rains did fall
On his arid, parched and hard baked clay,
When Adam stirred from sleep, he did recall
This dream, the radiant dawn of life's new day.
His prayer's been answered, way down deep,
Refreshed his soul awakes from torpid sleep.

48

WHO AM I?

Adam heard within his heart, the Sage ask "why?"
Speaking from silence, his voice, so soft and clear,
"Ask yourself the greatest question 'who am I?'
You aren't just a body, insentient thing of fear,
But Divine, a holy spark of sacred fire!
Quest within, search for that hidden flame,
Dive deep inside your Heart, enquire!
Until you find that ONE without a name!"

Adam felt free, his soul had found release,
Joyful calm and ease enwrapped his heart,
He now felt One, at home in perfect peace,
Losing the past, to carve a fresh new start.
My the message of his dream, our hope renew,
Go seek your Self within! Know 'That' is true!

49

MEDITATION

Renouncing all attachments, stuck to things
Like ivy tendrils cling to prison wall,
We bend the ear to hear a clarion call,
"Rest in the flame of Self our Phoenix sings!
"This is your natural state" the church bell rings!
"Dive deep in Consciousness of Being
To become the Light of effortless seeing
That I Am That I Am!" The bird sprouts wings
To inwardly soar and safely nest in Heart,
Released from snares, the properties of sense,
Now unveils our Natural Godlike part
Within, and like that Light rests in blissful ease.
So regain that 'One' illumined, from whence
We strayed, then come home in perfect peace.

50

PERFECT LIFE

The key to Perfect Life dwells deep in one's Self,
We must achieve perfection ourselves to live one.
And 'Know The Self' biding in the heart as the Sun.
Effort's essential to move from powerless puppet elf
To Sage, and escape hard fate of death and birth.
Like Phoenix, soul must rise from jet black ash
Of past lives, to strive with all her might and worth,
And shed all our latent accumulated trash,
By totally surrendering sad ego-mind
To the Sat-Guru dwelling deep in the heart,
Then with keen Self Enquiry, we shall find
His Great Power makes its graceful start.
Hail the glorious Sun blazing deep within,
Ready to free us ever more from worldly sin!

51

HARMONY DIVINE

Love's harmony lies in the sweet unstruck music,
Heard in the spiritual heart by those whose ears,
Are tuned into this subtle sacred angelic art,
And hear ethereal rhythms from galactic spheres.

There are no words to describe this awesome sound.
Once heard Jericho Walls of selfishness fall down,
And blissful inner feelings all in unison resound
With holy joy, bestowing love's most precious crown.

A deaf mute deprived of hearing and vocal speech,
Prayed to hear the magic of a chanting human voice.
God in His mercy, which he always grants to each,
Cured his ailment so the poor boy could now rejoice.
The highest form of music to him was then revealed,
By such harmony divine, the blessed lad was healed.

52

BRAHMAN

We Love Atman Brahman dwelling in our spiritual heart,
Self is indeed a tremendous awesome wondrous Power;
It fills ones inner breast with happiness, to impart
Joy, peace, and solace every moment, every hour.
All is well, very well, unfolding as preordained,
We trust in that Great Power, by Brahman its maintained!

He who knows 'That', the Perfect Supreme Being hidden
Dwelling in the sacred Heart Cave, and we reach Him there,
If we dive way down deep and find that as we're bidden,
To Realise Self as Brahman, that embraces everywhere!

The Power of Brahman is beyond verbal description,
It is Consciousness Awareness, Absolute and pure,
Sheer Existence, Reality, Bliss that shall ever endure,
Without any boundary, limit or spatial restriction.

53

RAIN

Thank God for morning's dew-drenched emerald lawn,
And the gentle rain that waters harvest fields,
That fills the mountain's sacred rivers so forlorn,
And aids all gardeners to gain rich floral yields.

The fresh spring water quenches dry thirst of man,
It cleanses all it reaches with its liquid hand,
This heavenly element maintains our days many a span
Of time. For the grace of rain our gratitude is ever grand.

In the desert of life, treading on dry sands of time,
Dwell blue oases of Truth to quench soul's dire need;
We bathe in sweet temple waters, a sacred rite divine,
To purify. Our earnest quest for Truth He'll ever feed.

Welcome the rain by singing hymns of holy joy,
A flood of God-Love which shall never ever cloy.

54

ARUNACHALA SIVA

Almighty mountain, emblem of the Self!
Red ruby stone, radiant with holy light,
Unborn, deathless , sacred sound of Aum ,
Near, as God, you're dear, inside my heart,
Abundantly showering, true love and grace.

Consciousness-absolute's power unfolds,
Helping devotees of Great Lord Ramana.
At your call, he came to dwell and teach
Lifting the world's burden from all who knelt
And prayed to wake from grey dream of life.

Surrendering at your feet, oh Lord!
I am the Self ! you loudly call, to all,
Victory over demonic ego-mind!
A lmighty mountain, emblem of the Self!

55

SURRENDER

I unconditionally surrender,
My body, my heart, my mind and my soul,
And all earthly possessions to You,
My dearly beloved Sat-Guru,
Always with me, eternally true.

I give up false sense of doership,
Your soft lotus feet are mine to worship,
My mischievous monkey-mind's surrendered.
My fervent faith is constant, ever whole,
Sworn and vowed, undoubted through and through.
Egotism lies shattered, broken and rendered.So this promise to
you I gladly send,
To complete my sadhana of 'Who Am I'
That will carry me to freedom before I die!

56

FIRMEST FAITH

Find firmest Faith in one's Sat-Guru deep in the heart,
His force of Self will quieten down meandering mind;
Peaceful joy, and paternal love, we'll quickly find.
That's all one needs to try, in order to impart
Self Knowledge, great miraculous, majestic art,
Which sets alight a magic life, ready to unwind.
Gracious virtues all unfold, most merciful and kind;
Mind's struck down by Realisation's sudden lightning dart!

Sadhak struggled hard to climb the upward mountain way,
To the peak of Arunachala's state for which he yearned.
Through grace he came upon a wise and humble Sage one day,
Who said "by persistence and effort you have justly earned,
The right to Liberation and enjoy sweet eternal peace,
From Self Enquiry and Surrender you never once did cease"!

57

BEAUTY POINTS TO FREEDOM

Golden sunflowers prank the river bank,
Deep blue waters flow briskly, like the dream
Of life, which the grateful heart shall thank
Heaven, for the stunning beauty of her scene.

As Beauty is the stepping stone to God;
The restless mind will hush in silent awe,
In thrall of lush green sward, growing from the clod
Of Earth, that opens up for soul a door,

To enter into union with all 'That' sees,
Straight away to our Being's inner core.
Bowing, the body bends in motion with the trees,
Soul prays for breeze to waft her to Nirvana's shore.

Iron mind's no longer imprisoned by its walls,
Proud arrogant ego topples down and falls.

58

WALKING ON WATER

Walk calmly on stormy world's restless waves,
Tossing and turbulent in a violent ocean,
Be free of the 'I am the body' notion;
In this way our Great Sage's teaching will save
Us from that treacherous egotistic knave,
Who stole God's role in soul's endless motion,
With worthless desires and pleasures keen to crave.
Dwelling in one's blissful Self is the supreme emotion!

Bold swimmer saw a tidal wave ahead,
Fearless he thought it prudent just to float,
Rather than brave tempest waves instead.
He survived like a strong well crafted boat,
And soon reached that heavenly other shore,
Where he dwelt blissfully there, for ever more!

59

UNCONDITIONAL SURRENDER

Surrender egotistic notion of 'I' and 'mine',
There's no such person there, mind's a bird's nest of thoughts,
A delusion by which we've been snared and caught;
True Self Knowledge Teaching, flowing from the Divine,
Says 'surrender the 'phantom me' and all shall be fine!
Trapped mind will no longer feel fright or fraught'.
This is what all Great Sages emphatically taught!
So there's no need to worry, be pained or to pine.

The Master said "whenever child, you utter 'I',
I walk, I talk, I squawk, I balk, ad infinitum,
You can be sure that you're telling one huge lie!
You're not the author of actions or their sum,
When you truly know 'That' you'll rest finally free,
Blissfully dwelling in Brahman, for all eternity"!

60

ALL IS ONE

The See-er, the seeing and the seen are One,
And all that we see is Bhagavan Ramana,
Pure Consciousness-Sat Chit Ananda!
In our heart shines a light, bright as the sun.
Ramana is our Sat-Guru; He's second to none!
Through His Grace, He'll save us from samsara,
And lead us to the bliss of Great Nirvana.
With Faith, all duties, by Him will be done,
There's no more worry, anxiety or care,
All responsibilities are well carried out,
No more dire depression or dark despair.
So with one voice, give a triumphant shout!
Om Namah Bhagavate Sri Ramanayah!
Adore Him! Om Shivayah Arunachala!

61

EQUANIMITY

Why worry about anything in life,
Thinking it be either pleasure or pain?
Where's the need ever to cry or complain,
Where's anything now like wrongful strife?
Guru does all for us, like a kind loving wife.
He knows what is best, there's no need to explain.
Leave it to him, keep calm, all anxiety is vain.
He'll cut that binding knot with Enquiry's knife!

Pilgrim went by train on a railroad track,
The fool was bearing his baggage on his head,
Instead of loading it on the luggage rack.
Se when we climb the mountain path, we're led
To give all our burden into good Guru's care,
We trust Him more than this world would ever dare!

62

SUNLIGHT

From darkness God spoke; "let there be light"! and there was
light.
To Earth he gave his mighty white hot fire named Sun,
A mass of vast atomic power that's outdone by none,
Warming his planets by day and cooling them by night,
All circling round that mammoth majestic sight.
A holy circuit around their Guru done,
They then finish their annual pilgrim's run,
As that gigantic solar force blazes on and on!

That Sun is macrocosm of our Real Self unborn,
Which shines as microcosm in every human heart,
Alas it is obscured by malign habits forlorn,
Its blazing light fails to reach the blinkered soul,
But Enquiry and Surrender, will make one whole,
And divine wisdom to the errant soul impart.

63

OH TO HELL O

"This above all to thine own Self be true,
Then thou cans't not be false to any man".
"This is the stuff that dreams are made of"! Who
Knows 'That', will awaken from sleep and can
Arise as Self reborn, 'That' is his essence too,
Rather than living like some Caliban,
Ape-man wallowing in his mental stew.
For the immortal bard knew God's master plan.

The tragedy of Lear is real inverted,
And Regan is anger; all anagrams
Like Goneril's religion; so the poet converted
Subtle meanings into his plays for man.
'Mercy flows from heaven like gentle rain',
He shakes his spear of truth again and again.

64

CRIME PREVENTION

Ego dresses up as policeman to trap a thief,
To catch the crook red handed and give us great relief;
That's achieved by plunging deep into the heart,
The wicked scoundrel falls when his base we start
To touch, and Realisation comes to all who dive;
Then from spiritual death we rise again alive!
So Self Enquiry will destroy the criminal mind,
That our Sat-Guru taught and that is what we find!

A wicked burglar broke into a pilgrim's house,
To rob his essential substance like a hungry mouse
Steals the larder cheese. It needs some watchful cats,
To put a final end to thieving mice and rats.
The cat is ever alert and constantly aware;
Awareness guards the heart from all that steals in there!

65

HOLY ARUNACHALA

Hail Arunachala, sacred hill of Grace!
Our beloved Bhagavan's blessed home,
Lucent ruby jewel beneath a saphire dome;
You know that all is perfect and in place,

Auspicioness flows from your awesome space,
Radiating the mystical throb of Aum,
Until pilgrims find no more need to roam,
No more deprived of your roseate face,
Absolute wonder for a sad and weary world.
Compassionate friend of every devotee,
Holy hill where Brahman's power is here unfurled,
And by your grace, imprisoned souls fly free,
Love and salvation is there waiting for all,
And You save those who earnestly heed your call!

66

I AM THAT I AM

God spoke to Moses midst thorns of crackling fire,
He told him "I AM THAT I AM, that's my sacred name.
King David chanted psalms and strummed upon his lyre,
He said "Be still and know that I am God, they're just the same".
I AM THAT is stated by the great Advaita Sages,
Who've recognized the Truth throughout the many ages.
Consciousness- Awareness, free from vain tendencies and pure,
Is that 'I AM'; the key to Jnana which always must endure.
So Hebrew prophets and Hindu Sages all agree,
To rest in one's I AMNESS is the best way to be free!

Mohammad, great prophet of Allah, wisely said,
"God is closer than one's breathing, hands and feet".
If one remembers 'THAT I AM', then one is quickly led,
To a life of wholeness, fulfilled and quite complete;

67

HEART DIVING

Dive into the heart with strong tenacity,
Intense love, patience and alacrity;
Such practice must surely end in Jnana,
So said great Holy Sage, Lord Ramana.
He gave the Eki Sloka* to the Muni
The Kavankanti who was like Ganapati,
Brother to God Skanda, the son of Shiva,
Who was reborn on earth as Sage Ramana
To bring us the blessing of atma vichara.

Such is the power of this great sadhana,
That egotism is removed and the Sun of Jnana
Shines forth to enlighten the sad ignorant jiva,
That's the great gift from Sri Bhagavan Ramana,
Who came on Earth to guide mankind to Jnana!

THE EKI SLOKA*

"IN THE INMOST CORE, THE HEART
SHINES AS BRAHMAN ALONE,
AS I-I, THE SELF AWARE.
ENTER DEEP INTO THE HEART
BY SEARCH FOR SELF, OR DIVING DEEP,
WITH BREATH UNDER CHECK.
THUS ABIDE EVER IN ATMAN."

This verse hangs above Sri Bhagavan Ramana Maharshi's couch
in the New Hall engraved in gold on black basalt.

68

ARUNACHALA RAMANA

Bhagavan is my safe and sole refuge,
To save me from delusion's stormy deluge.
I open the gates of my heart so the King
Of Glory can come in! With love, I sing
To the Self, inside my heart as Ramana.
Who gave us the gift of atma vichara.

I surrender at his sweet lotus feet,
Offering my mind as sacrifice complete!
I pray this gift shall soon be accepted,
Or I will waste away if it's neglected.
Om Namah Bhagavate Sri Ramanayah!
Om Namah Shivayah! beloved mantra.
By diving persistently into the heart,
I trust Self Knowledge, He shall soon impart!

69

SACRIFICE

Place ego-mind on the fiery flame of sacrifice,
In your spiritual heart abiding on the right.
The fool's heart's on the left as the sagely bright
Ecclesiastes wisely said, to be precise.
Bhagavan confirmed that Truth too, clearly and concise.
'There dwells the Sun of Self, its shining blazing light,
Is darkly veiled by vasanas, black as night.
Remove them by surrender and enquiry. That's my Sage advice!'

God told A Brahman to sacrifice his only son
Isaac, a deed of devotion and surrender,
But compassionately, the Lord said "none
Of your kith and kin do you need to render,
Just circumcise your righteous heart instead,
Then demon ego will surely drop down dead"!

70

WAKE UP!

Mad monkey mind is made of mundane schemes:
Should I do this or that? It plans and plans
Pastimes, to occupy its restless hands.
But all these plans are but fantastic dreams,
For man cannot do! and so it seems,
All this talk of should and ought, just lands
In crass confusion, and tightens bondage bands.

The Way of Self Knowledge comes in gleams,
To enlighten man, and wake him up from sleep,
And abandon all this stupid waste of time!
The sacred task for jiva's sake is to keep
Up sadhana, away from that wicked crime
Of wasting life away in dubious distractions,
Devoured by paltry pleasures and attractions

71

GREAT TRICKS OF GRACE

Does Almighty God play tricks and games of grace?
Misunderstood by man's puny rational mind?
The answer's surely yes! Great Sages find
That much happens beyond that tiny space
Of weak human knowledge, and at such a pace
That can't be fathomed by the spiritually blind.
God's most merciful, compassionate and kind,
Have faith that all his acts are simply t grace in place.

An earnest pilgrim had an accident one day,
He fell and broke his leg while climbing on a gate;
"This was a trick of grace", his Guru then did say,
"Because it averted a much harder graver fate".
Tricks of Grace are well beyond our human ken,
Rely on Grace's great abundance, and never worry then!

72

STORMY SEA

Let's not be drowned in a stormy sea of words,
Struggling, paddling, to keep one's soul afloat,
Praying for rescue from our Guru's boat.
Mind is worse than a flock of parrot birds,
The voice of reason's blocked and rarely heard.
Keeping quiet is much wiser than to quote
Mental chat, which clouds the Self and will promote
Staying in samsara, which is most absurd!

Sadhak's mind kept muttering all day long,
Unable to control his monkey mind,
He knew that habit was very, very wrong;
But a way to check the pest he couldn't find.
The Sat-Guru came and said "watch your breath
And its flow, mind will slow, and speed vile ego's death!

73

LAMP OF NON DUAL KNOWLEDGE

Life's a hurdy-gurdy, set to be reborn again;
A great game of hallucination and dark delusion,
A carousel carnival of crass illusion,
Tuned to chords of circumstance as its refrain
'Bewitched, bothered and bewildered', it's not that plain!
So what's the cause of such confounded confusion?
Past life tendencies concoct a cocktail diffusion;
The world's drama's a dream, we're driven insane.
A mad mixture of magic maya and monkey mind;
A mistake is made, to think the world is real.
But on metaphysical enquiry we soon shall find,
It's a dubious deception, all we see, hear and feel!
Read Lamp of Non Dual Knowledge* and you'll learn how,
This world is mentally created, right here and now!

*Advaita Bhoda Deepika

74

MORE TRICKS OF GRACE

Self Realisation is a waiting game,
If it happened too quickly it might kill.
The nervous system must be tuned until
It can bear full force of Consciousness, same
As Pure Awareness, moksha is its name.
So there must be patience, and time we'll fill
With sadhana, to keep the soul from ill,
Then egotism will fall down, limp and lame!

Sadhak asked his Guru about tricks of grace,
He answered "They're sent to save us from disaster,
And not understood by mind, they efface
Danger when we rush much faster and faster;
While safety lies in being peacefully calm,
Then sadhak will never come to any harm!"

75

ENDLESS DISTRACTION

Mischievous monkey mind plays an endless game
To relieve the worldly boredom of its state,
And end the painful headache, that's ordained by fate:
So pursuing pleasure, sensation or fame,
Without fear or favour, shame, remorse or blame,
Is mind's way, this toilsome trouble to abate,
Brazen and impatient, it has no time to wait.
Carnal enjoyment is its constant clammy claim.
All this woeful waste of energy and time,
Would better be spent in practical sadhana.
That's the needed Holy Task to try that's prime,
So said Great Sage Sri Bhagavan Ramana,
For mature souls this must be their chief aim,
And they'll reach the Power of that Holy Name!

76

MY SAT GURU APPEARS

"I'm but an appearance in your life dream my dear,
Don't be afraid, I'm not some feisty phantom ghost,
In fact I shall become your precious teaching host;
So there's no need for any anxious qualms or fear,
I'm your Sat-Guru sent to bring you much cheer;
In time you'll come to love me the very most
Of the many men idly mistaken for a post;
I'll teach you Self Enquiry and free you from here.
Your Guru appears like a lion in your dream,
To awaken you from the nightmare of samsara.
I'm not exactly what I look like or seem,
In fact my name is Sri Bhagavan Ramana!
I'll free you from your iron prison of mind,
A loving more helpful friend you never will find"!

77

WHORE HOUSE SCORNED

A respectable pilgrim eyed a prostitute
Eating dog-flesh en route to her house of whores,
He thought, as she flounced through the brothel door,
Being a very fine man of high repute,
He'd avoid that bitch like poisoned fruit.
But such is the case with any soul, what's more,
Who harbours the 'I am the body notion', for
Who scorns that lie, like dog flesh, is freed and astute.

A sadhak walked by a plague-ridden town,
He soon turned round and raced quickly away,
He knew if he stayed he'd soon be struck down,
And his life would end, on that fateful day!
That town is like the 'I am the body notion',
Its rejection surely leads to Self's shoreless ocean!

78

THY WILL BE DONE

Even when our God seems to be unwilling,
His will is still my affirmative will!
The duty of man is just be still,
Instead of letting monkey mind go killing
Realisation of the Self, and then filling
Soul with idle chatter that works for ill;
It makes one's worldly dream a bitter pill
To swallow and send the senses reeling.
Keeping quiet is a much wiser feeling,
And will lead to real freedom if maintained,
So peace and bliss are in the Heart retained,
And man lives in happiness and endless joy,
A state of Being which can never cloy.
Existence- Awareness- Love, is that state of Being!

79

MOTHER MAYA'S MAGIC PICTURE SHOW

This so-called world you view, dear aspiring friend,
Is a crazed creation of one's ignorant mind;
It's produced by latent tendencies, that we find
From many previous lives, and in the end,
It's like a dream at night in which we pretend
We believe as real; but it's nothing of the kind!
It's like a film, and the spool will soon unwind,
So pictures on the screen 'twill swiftly send.
Sages term it 'instantaneous creation',
It depends on the seer; but who is seeing?
So we're trapped in fanciful fascination,
Tricked by coloured pictures that mind's revealing.
This world's a product of one's imagination
And we're deceived by such a strange sensation.

80

DREAM HALL OF MIRRORS

What we need to do is inwardly turn
And Self Enquire; that's the best of all!
Then turn to Bhagavan, and in surrender fall,
Then watch the flame of Agni slowly burn
All vile vasanas away; ego it will spurn!
Don't be perplexed in the Dream Figure Hall
Of Mirrors, which fill the seeming world, but call
For Grace! through effort, Moksha one can earn!

Sadhak was perplexed by figures in life's dream,
His Sad Guru said to him " my dearest son,
Forget all those people, they only seem
As real; pray turn within and wake up upon
Your bed, forever end that dread samsara"!
Soon he was free, thanks to great Lord Ramana!

81

SACRIFICE

Offer 'mind' on the funeral pyre of sacrifice,
In one's spiritual heart abiding on the right.
"The fool's heart's on the left" as wisely bright
Ecclesiastes firmly stated, to be quite precise.
Bhagavan echoed him, most clearly and concise;
"There dwells the Sun of Self, but its shining light
Is darkly veiled by malign vasanas black as night,
Remove them by Surrender, that's my sage advice"!

God told A Brahman to sacrifice his only son
Isaac, a deed of devotion and surrender,
But then compassionately the Lord said "None
Of your kith and kin do you need to render;
Just circumcise your righteous heart instead,
Then demonic ego will surely drop down dead"!

82

CHARTRES

GLORY OF GOD'S GOSPEL

THE GLORY of God's Gospel glows with light;
Pilgrim sees growing from green on the ground
A tall temple of stone hewn high on a mound.
Her sculptured craft astounds his purblind sight,
He falls down, surrendered, with all of his might.
He's awed by the magic charms of her sound,
Angels chant psalms, stained windows shine bright.
It's New Jerusalem, the City of God re-found.

Each niche tells a legend set in tinted glass,
Radiant rainbow hue, sparkling like dew,
The inward mind knows her message to be true.
Pilgrim feels healed by the visions that pass,
His Soul wakes up, no beam blurs his eye,
Heart's upraised by her spires, high in the sky.

83

HER STEEPLES ASPIRE

Her steeples aspire like arrows aimed at God;
Prayers assault her vaults, for heaven's sought.
The soul's inflamed to blaze in its earthy clod,
By Saints, who from her oaken pulpit taught.
A medieval miracle, mighty marvel, to behold!
Amazed by the maze on her limestone floor,
Many parables on her painted panes unfold,
We stand in awe before her portal door.

To calmly comprehend the art of Chartres,
Where cryptic Christian chrisms are unveiled.
Start to chart her craft inside your heart.
In such masterly masonry, much is revealed.
Her stained glass windows glow like precious gems,
Showing celestial scenes from which truth doth stem.

84

AH CHARTRES!

Ah Chartres! 'mystère merveille', enigmatic book
Of God's creation, you're an emblematic sign.
Architectonic is your binding, majestic, divine,
Your pages etched on alchemic glass. So look
For graven keys in carved and buttressed nook.
Christ points the way the saints and martyrs took,
There were miracles, wan water turned to wine,
Wonder of Chartres, may your beauty e'er be mine.

On slabs of limestone lies a cryptic maze
Soul's riddle, the puzzle in which she's caught.
Once dancing here, a Master Templar taught
His Masons, the measured steps to freedom's ways.
In Chartre's stone arches, clues are given,
Sacred tunes for hymns, wend their way to heaven.

85

DIG DOWN DEEP

Dig down deeply, dive in one's Self to find
The Chartres Cathedral inside the inner heart,
The real temple ever bides behind the mind.
Stab the stony slabs of sleep, and start
To plunge within the cloister well, hold breath
In one's sanctum sanctorum in the east transept.
Notre Dame de Chartres mirrors the One inside,
The Light Of The World behind the door, doth hide.

So step beyond the Gothic shades, uncover all!
The Kingdom Of Heaven shines within, not out,
Real Chartres shines within one's heart, so turn about
Into the Self within, where God's Grace doth fall,
Chartres Cathedral, miracle for all to see,
A pilgrimage there may well enlighten thee.

86

HIDDEN TREASURE

The Great Power within is our hidden treasure,
The pearl of great price beyond any measure.
 It 's God, it's Divine, it's the Sat- Guru within,
Surrender to 'That' and end gross error of sin
Of wandering perverted mind, which ever clouds
The pure shining Self with a myriad of shrouds.
 Surrendering to that Power is our holy task,
It will grant liberation if we earnestly ask.

A pilgrim was plodding on the mountain way,
Self enquiring, surrendering everyday.
All of a sudden after effort filled years,
A voice spoke into his welcoming ears,
A Power spoke from deep in his heart,
"Walk on! Self Realisation, I shall soon impart!

APOTHEOSIS

THE FLOOD OF SHIVA BLISS

A free versification of selected stanzas from Shankara's great epic, Saundaryalahari

87

GREAT LORD SHIVA

May this, my most humble submission be,
To that one great auspicious Deity;
Great Lord Shiva of everlasting fame,
Quintessence of all Jnana is His Name!
He sports on His crown, a silver crescent moon,
Ornament for Uma, such a beauteous boon,
The ripe fruit of harsh severe penitence,
Bestowing His bounteous beneficence.
He wills all devotees to be ever blessed,
And enjoy full noble lives of happiness.
He always appears in the surrendered heart,
Glimpsed His presence will never ever depart.
He showers all three worlds with perfect love,
A merciful blessing, mighty Grace from above.

88

VICTORY

Victory to the powers of Great Lord Shiva!
Which flow from the blessings of His kind
Removal of sorrow from my mundane mind;
He frees me from great grief of samsara
To know soul's lagoon flooded by Nirvana.
Such awakening from hypnotic sleep we find
Are streams that cleanse the soul, they wind
Through dense mud and mire of false ajnana.
They cause destruction of pain and sorrow,
We live in the present, no fear for tomorrow.
We thank Shiva with all our might and main,
Chanting His praises for sacred is His Name.
We read the miracles of His great life story,
And bathe in the light of His effulgent glory.

89

WORSHIP

I worship Lord Shiva with all of my heart,
Unknowable through the Vedas! For a start
He destroyed those tyrannical cities three,
Made of iron, silver and gold; to set free
Causal and subtle bodies. Veda His bow,
Agni His barb, Vishnu His well honed arrow;
His feather, the dreaded Lord Yama,
His faithful charioteer, Great God Brahma.
He's primordial, sighted by three eyes,
He's majestic and profoundly wise.
His hair's a profusion of matted locks;
He wears a necklace of snakes, carved from rocks.
Gracious to every ardent devotee,
He's the God of souls, Lord of Divinity.

90

GODS HOLD SWAY

Myriads of Gods hold sway over the world,
And grant the prayers of the immature.
Even in dreams at night, I pray to be pure,
To my poor soul, high wisdom He's unfurled.
What I yearn for, is that He will insure
The worship of His lotus feet, to lure
My mind from grave sin, by senses hurled.
This steady worship of His lotus feet
Is not easy, even for those sitting near
Him, with hearts full of love complete,
Having firm faith and freedom from fear,
Yet fickle mind feels feeble and effete.
It was difficult for Vishnu and Lord Brahma,
Even Sita, Hanuman, and great Prince Rama.

91

LEGALISTIC CODES

I'm not well versed in legalistic codes,
Nor in learned philosophic tomes,
From sciences, my mind always roams.
Neither in art of music and poetic odes,
Nor reading texts, burdened by heavy loads
Do I ever feel comfortably at home.
I please Kings no more than an impish gnome,
I'm as little use as a sweeper of roads.
Save this wretched soul through Thy mighty grace!
Omniscient, greatly famed, Oh Holy One,
I pray to see my own original face,
Resplendent as Thy bright effulgent Sun.
Only Thee Lord Shiva can save my errant soul,
To know my own Real Self and make me whole!

92

LOGIC CHOPPING

Whether it be a pot or heavy lump of clay,
Or the microcosmic atom in my breath,
Whether it be smoke, fire or mountain way,
Will any serve as a cure for painful death?
I'm only blocking love by logic chopping,
I must bow to praise great Lord Shiva's feet,
But monkey mind keeps dropping off, hopping,
Instead of abiding in His bliss replete.
The heavy means of reason and causation,
Will never take me to Self Realisation,
Instead they lead to endless frustration,
A kind of morbid mental perturbation.
I must take refuge in Lord Shiva's grace
Inside my heart, True Saviour of the race.

93

LORD SUPREME

Let me rest at your feet, my Lord Supreme,
Soft as the beautiful blue lotus flower.
Let my speech, with all its might and power,
Be prayer to awaken, from life's sad dream,
And constantly illuminate my inner scene.
Then uttering your praise, I'll never cower
With fear, or lose the faith, by which Thou endower
My soul by light from Thine effulgent gleam.
Let my palms be clasped, in worship of Thee,
My hearing tuned to the words of Thy story,
My mind in meditation and ever free,
My eyes resting on Thy formless glory.
So through which other senses, will I learn
To become worthy, and Thy grace to earn?

94

THE SPELL OF MAYA

Oh Great God Shiva, Lord of many Souls,
As one thinks nacre, looks like silver in a shell,
Or water mixed with flour, looks like milk as well,
A glass bead bauble appears as a crystal bowl,
A mirage we think is just a watering hole;
So the fool, destined for yet another hell,
Worships other than what is Thee; the spell
Of Maya that deceives, Oh Lord of the Whole!
The rope we perceive is a venomous snake,
And the stone dog we imagine to be real.
We mistake a man for a scarecrow's stake,
And what we touch seems solid when we feel.
The mind is under a constant delusion,
Save us Lord Shiva from such illusion!

95

LORD OF ARUNA

Lord of Aruna! One swims in a deep tank,
Walks in a fearful, empty jungle wood,
Climbs a mountain peak where fresh air is good,
Pick pretty posies by a river bank,
That fool doesn't know how to give Thee thanks!
All one needs to do as one truly should,
To worship Thy lotus feet to be understood.
You do not need to be decked with flowers,
You're already the beautifully sublime,
These outer forms waste many precious hours;
The true sacrifice which is really prime,
Is to offer one's mind to the Self in the heart,
That's all Shiva asks, from the very start,
To lead us to Selfhood divine and sublime!

96

HUMAN BIRTH

Let there be birth as a human being,
Or a God in some ethereal sphere,
A high mountain where the clouds float near,
Or forest fox from huntsmen ever fleeing,
Or mosquito blood juice always stealing.
Cow, whose lush green grass is ever dear,
Worm, who through mud does craftily steer,
Or bird who through azure sky flies wheeling.
What is this compared to sporting in bliss
From great Lord Shiva's benefaction?
Receiving the grace of sweet Parvati's kiss,
All for poor jiva's endless satisfaction.
If we offer our mind, each night and morn,
Does it matter into which body we're reborn?

97

LET ME BE

Let me be a student, humble as can be,
Or the proud house holder of a home,
An ascetic, plastic as a garden gnome,
Or any other form, as it pleases Thee.
What use is this on the path to liberty?
Oh Sambhu, when the Heart- lotus is Thine
I become yours, no longer 'me' or 'mine';
One's burden of life is Thy responsibility.
Whether I dwell in town or mountain cave,
My mind will always wander with me;
The solution Lord Shiva gives to save
And rest at peace, to be eternally free,
Is to surrender ego mind to my own dear Self,
And slay that demonic self-centred elf.

98

ENDLESS SPECULATION

Let one live in damp jungle or in fire,
Or on Himalayan mountain peak,
Or whatever place a man may seek.
In a palace, to which great Kings aspire,
Or fabled lands of which the pilgrims speak
Of Vedic Indian, or Platonic Greek;
Of endless speculation we soon tire.
Of what use is such wasteful living?
Instead prostrate at mighty Shiva's feet,
Endlessly renouncing, and freely giving
Back our minds in full surrender complete.
That's the only way to make us content,
Ego's false ignorance we need to relent,
And bathe in his grace ambrosial sweet.

99

SAVIOUR OF SOULS

Oh Saviour of wretched afflicted souls,
It is Thy duty to protect and guard me,
Thou whom art all compassion and mercy:
I'm blind, roasted over life's blazing coals,
I boast, foolishly hosting madcap goals,
And the weakest in mental strength Thou sees?

Pray grant me safe refuge and set me free!
I pray to abide in the heart with Thee.
Like some poor dove trapped in a gilded cage,
My soul pines to fly and roost at Thy feet;
Remove all my sins of anger and rage,

Help me renounce foul mind and rest complete.
Who's a better expert in the saving grace?
Lead me to the vision of my original face.

100

LORD OF SOULS

Oh Lord of Souls! art Thou not also Lord
And firm friend of the impoverished poor?
In earnest we pray, open wide Thy door
To the music of that merciful chord,
Which Thou can graciously well afford,
To heal our wounded hearts, so sore.
Aid us in practice to move closer toward
Thy Lotus feet and then walk on forward,
To Realisation of the Self for ever more.
All my sins should be forgiven by Thee,
This is the true duty of a loving father,
Willing to help his child, strive for liberty!
Or grant me protection, and play Thy part
Against those thieves, breaking into my Heart.

101

BE NOT INDIFFERENT

Lord, as Thou are not indifferent to my lot,
Why not destroy that grave decree of fate,
Before death comes, and alas it is too late,
That which makes me wilt. Hast Thou forgot
That unless you save me, there's a vile plot
Of desires set to invade me? pray don't forsake,
Your child before I reach Lord Yama's Gate,
And you've failed to sever my ganglion knot.
If you're powerless, how was Taraka's head,
Which cannot be plucked by a finger nail,
Cut by Thee as Skanda with nail tip instead?
I pray, Great Ramana, please don't fail.
Your child who tries so hard in this barren place,
Lies powerless without thy boundless grace

102

ALL PERVADING

Oh Master, whom art all pervading,
Either because of my merited deeds,
Or through compassion for my earthly needs;
Thou art immanently present, invading
Each fibre of my soul, not evading
But helping me, when my sad heart bleeds;
For you've truly sown salvation's seeds
The fruits of which are now parading.
How am I to reach Thy sweet lotus feet?
The whole galaxy of Gods press forward
In their eagerness to respect and greet
Thy gracious Self, paying obeisance toward
Thee, with the splendour of Thy golden crown,
Preventing poor me alas, from bending down.

103

BOON BESTOWER

Oh Shiva! Thou art the boon giver supreme,
Vishnu and the lesser Gods call upon Thee,
They hold their place through Thy generosity;
How great is Thy grace, and yet we scheme
With increased desires in this crazy dream.
When will you destroy pernicious petty 'me',
Through thy gaze of peaceful clemency?
From your dazzling light cast me a single beam.
The Gods pray for you to uphold their gains,
Blessed benefactor of all sentient Beings,
Strengthen and fasten my slack mental reins,
Unite see-er, and seen with all my seeings.
I depend on Thee Lord Shiva for Thy grace,
Accept me, and my false ego pray efface.

104

SUFFERING OF BIRTH AND DEATH

Is it to benefit great Great Lord Brahma
That you won't remove my anguish and pain?
Full of despicable desires and shame,
This endless suffering in dark samsara
Even leads to door of some crooked Rajah,
An endless storm of troubles, all in vain,
Without virtue, for my poor soul to gain.
Oh what a wretched wicked palaver!
Inform me, oh great Lord Shiva, I pray
If all this grief is only for Thy pleasure,
We shall be gracefully blessed, I say.
I beg for justice as you shall measure,
None of the dark decrees of fate for ill,
Have any true validity before Thy will.

105

THE MENDICANT

Oh Shiva, with bare skull as begging bowl,
Thou art an all pervading, mendicant!
My mind roams the desert of discontent,
Dances on the breast hills of female souls,
Leaps wildly on many mad strange goals,
Branch to branch, where desire will soon torment.
Inconstant is this monkey mind Thou sent
To fight against, and learn firm sense control.
Taking this mind as an offering of alms,
Bind it tightly with Thy cord of devotion,
And tie it well, beneath your loving arms,
As I sail across life's stormy ocean.
Lord Shiva save me from the terror of my mind!
Thou art the Truest Guru I could ever find.

106

SLAYER OF DEMONS

Oh, Slayer of Demons, like Manmatha,
Thou art worshiped by earnest devotees.
All pervading One, please enter with these,
And Thy Goddess consort, beauteous Uma,
Into the bright tent of my mental maya,
That boasts free will; a central pole to seize
The ropes of heroic virtues that please,
And can be eased through this dread samsara.
That shining tent is multi-toned and hued,
Painted with lotuses, pink, blue and white,
They glow like beacons in the black of night,
Moved daily through highways, and imbued
With prayer for Thy great victory, Jai!
That enlivens me throughout my day.

107

MASTER THIEF

Oh Shankara! Oh skilful master thief!
Magnificent ever pervading One!
This arch villain of my mind speeds along,
Having fallen prey, beyond all belief,
To amassing great wealth without relief
From greedy desire , committing much wrong,
Rifling homes, to which the rich belong.
All this crime causes me remorse and grief.
How can I bear this unscrupulous knave?
Having brought him under Thy firm control,
Grant me thy Grace, my impure soul pray save,
Oh blessed Lord, please make me Thine, and Whole!
Accept that I my pure Self is innocent,
Oh merciful Lord Shiva, I repent, repent!

108

SAVE ME IMMORTAL SHIVA

Ever all-pervading One, Oh Shankara!
I perform Thy worship, pray grant poor me,
Realisation now, immediately!
Should Thou grant me the throne of Lord Brahma,
Or God Vishnu as fruit of my Puja,
I would bear more pain of taking the body
Of bird or beast, for sake of being free
And bathing in bliss of blest Nirvana.
How can I bear this agony and pain,
My auspicious beloved Guru Lord?
I beg you over and over again,
With all the strength and might I can afford,
Save me, immortal Shiva, I pray, I pray
I love you as my own dear Self, in every way.

SELECTED POEMS

FIRE

Almighty God spoke on high to holy Moses,
From a bed of thorns, like our prickly world.
In compassion He mercifully proposes
To set that bush on fire, and then unfurled

His great message 'I AM' of awesome power!
To burn the dross which clouds the errant soul,
And fill with joy and bliss man's every hour,
To recreate his life and make it whole.

This fire was One that eats all other fire,
A fire that burns all things be they dry or wet,
A fire that glows in snow and ice to inspire
A mode of fire, like a crouching lion all set

To reveal himself in many forms and names,
That can never ever perish or expire,
Shining and roaring mid life's strange games,
Blazing, sparkling a fiercesome white hot fire

That flies and fans madly in stormy gale,
That burns without wood or any other fuel,
That renews itself each day never to fail:
Fire, man's great emblem of his pledged renewal.

CHECKMATE

Cruel King Ego stands with his haughty band,
Ready to wage the chequered game of fate,
Queen Truth waits with army straight at hand,
Battle's to be staged before it gets too late.

Black King wore a blindfold as dark as night,
His mob is ready to fight and mate white Queen,
Fair Queen shone brightly like morning light,
She gathers in her might, surveys the battle scene.

She makes first move and sends a centre pawn
To reign o'er the board and commence attack,
The Black King blocked it with regal scorn,
White Queen sent a Knight to lead her pack.

The game progressed 'til locked in fight,
Queen gained the upper hand and he resigned,
It was the triumph over wrong by right
Defeating the wandering perverted mind.

If there's a moral to this chequered tale,
Win or lose, just enjoy the royal game,
Persistence and practice will never fail,
For no thought force ever goes in vain.

WHAT IS

You cannot say 'yea!' to the world, and miss out bits,
An amalgam of some near misses and straight hits,
A wet cement-mix for bricks of the world to fix together,
Through foul, beastly and brilliant fine weather.

God knows what He wants even if we don't understand,
It's His universe and proceeds as He's precisely planned.
Just accept and welcome all that happens as His great plan,
And then dear friends we end up a better woman or man.

Let's be born afresh from the burnt out ashes of the past,
Die to all that has been, and joyfully start anew,
All that happened was only for a time and cannot last,
What remained was a lesson from above, meant alone for you.

EGOMANIA

It would be good if one could write a perfect verse
Of Truth; a poem which expresses the reverse
Of falsity and illusion. Man is trapped in delusion,
Vast populations dwell in chronic confusion,
Because of a dire disease called egomania,
Stretching from Greenland right down to Australia.

Symptoms of egomania obscure Real Being,
The Knowledge of True Self without really feeling,
The pure bliss of consciousness awareness grace;
Realising 'That' as one's own original face,
Not the one we see in the silvered looking glass,
That idolatry is one through which we must pass.

The way to achieve this more blessed sacred state,
Is by Self Enquiry, before it is too late.
We enquire within through attention 'Who Am I?',
And persist resolutely before we die.
Then the perfect Poem is unveiled, to be only you,
Ones own pure loving Self, and "That" alone is true!

ARUNACHALA HILL OF GRACE

Parrots love to glean among ripening luscious fruits so fine,
But beware of little lemurs or there'll be no sparkling wine
Of ecstasy this morn, ushered in by radiant ruby dawn,
When prayer and meditation declare the soul's to be reborn.

Striding up the sacred roseate mountain path, laughing aloud,
Far away from the noisy, hurried, bustling maddening crowd,
While lucid dew drops, rainbow edged, grace the heavenly
scene,
Pilgrim laughs, striving hard to wake up from his daunting
dream

Of mundane life, which prisons sleeping mankind's worldly
throng.
So now he fills his lungs with air and sings a joyful song,
"Hara, hara, hara, maha deva, om namah shivayah!
All praise our great Sat-Guru beloved Bhagavan Ramanayah!

Let us prostate before his gentle soft lily lotus feet,
Then his boundless Grace will surely heal our weeping soul
complete,
And lead us to enlightening moksha through his penetrating
gaze,
Where we shall bathe in sat-chit-ananda all our blissful days.

Trust that great magnificent power which truly knows the way,
It thrives inside our own dear Self if we honour 'That' each day,
All will be well, very, very well, unfolding as it should,
Then we'll emerge free! laughing out of sad samsara's wood.

AURORA

The morning light of golden hue is born,
Proud cocks all crow in carillon call,
Dark's dispelled by red streaks of radiant dawn.

Hear choirs of birds carolling hymns for all,
To raise awareness up, as opening eyes
Greet a great new day. Waiting Soul grows tall.

Now wide awake, attention inward flies,
To find Self in Heart this blessed morn,
The Self, a blazing light that never dies.

A SONG OF UNITY

I am full as a mountain lake after the summer rain
That's fed the sacred stream and source of holy wisdom, love.
A fire sent by God to ignite His planet, from above.
The golden glow of heat on burnished plain
Gilding leaves on this march down pilgrim's lane;
Warming the earth, her gritty ochre clay,
Water, sea of mercy, so green and grey.
Air, the sweet breath of life that's free from pain,
Crystalline, beyond any loss or gain.
What does it mean to my Master, pure as a turtle dove?
This vast empty void, a deep abyss, the precious pearl
Of trial that poor pilgrim has to pay.

What of scripture, tracts, gospels and theological books?
The Lord's lurid library of commands and revelation;
A crore of scribbling comments with endless emendation,
Weighty tomes which cram cathedrals nook and crook
To surfeit, cawing like a craw of rooks.
What is self-knowledge, esoteric?
Pathology of mind, narcissistic?
Even when freed from the senses it looks
A hotchpotch prepared by the devil's cooks;
To titillate the senses to some novel sensation.
So what is freedom, vulgarised by folk-democratic?
But my Master who is One is truly aristocratic!

What is knowledge of truth, understanding, enlightenment
And ignorance, sleep, alienation, dark delusion
Or folly, dithering in a dream of world illusion?
Or freedom from bondage and attachment?
Are these questions the prime predicament?

What means ego? I thought, I conceit
Imprisoned by mind, one beds in self-deceit,
This is mine, a grasping temperament
For baubles, attractive but so vehement?
Or the form of self-consciousness to save from confusion,
To rescue soul from duality, its preordained defeat?
I pray for grace and mercy at my Master's tender feet.

I am without a central 'I-notion' resident at home,
There's no me to be elated or badly hurt by fear,
Pleased, perplexed, precious, pouting, proud, or simply here
To feel depressed, anxious. A soul free to roam
On inward seascape of bubbles, froth and foam.
So where is he who suffers, enjoys, acts,
Who has strong opinions and knows all facts?
The rising of thoughts under a cerebral dome,
What's this world? The trinket of an impish gnome?
Here and now there's no fictional person to jeer or leer,
For my Master, Dame Fortune's cards are neatly dealt in stacks,
Abidance in the heart, Real Self, no need for lofty tracts.

Seated in the temple shrine of the spiritual heart
Nestling on the dexter side of my heaving breast
Not on the left where the fleshly pump pulses in the chest,
Dwells 'I Am' which wakens Self to start.
Pondering, I question, what is the part
I play on life's stage and what is this world?
Who yearns for freedom from prison where hurled?
Oh what is oneness, truth and wisdom's art?
Into which God shot love's rose-flowered dart?
Who is bound or free as the honoured friend and conscious
guest?
Behind the nervous body-mind and now at last unfurled,
Space for a universe to happen in, lustrous and impearled.

Deep in my spiritual Heart, I am the One, unborn,
Uncaused, deathless, I am, uniquely perfect, new, absolutely
free!
I ask what is this tempestuous, stormy, troubled sea?
Where froth foams spuming from dusk to dawn,
On the ocean of Self lit by a fiery morn.
What is creation, world dissolution?
I ponder, and search for some solution.
Who and what is seeking? King, bishop or pawn
On this chequered emerald palace lawn?
What is the goal of seeking? Is it peace, freedom, liberty?
Who is the bold seeker who craves this final absolution?
Has he found any answer? An ultimate resolution!

I am pristine, pure as the driven Abyssinian snow
As a pellucid stream pouring from a pinnacle's height,
Chaste, flawless, stainless, without blame, blemish and wintry
white.
I trickle down the mountain valley's flow
Free! I'm curious, what is there to know?
By what dubious method is knowledge gained,
To what spurious end when it's attained?
I have no problems here, now or there below,
I've surmounted grief, all sorrow born of woe,
Simply stated, I know what is meant by both wrong and right.
Our universe by creation, preservation, is maintained
By grace of God and his mighty will, all creatures are sustained.

Here, awakened now, I am steady and perfectly still
As an adamantine rock in the restless ocean stands,
Unmoved by cyclonic gale, tidal wave or shifting sands,
What of oppositions, healthy or ill,
Pleasure, pain, to heal quickly or to kill;
Distraction, perturbation, meditation,

Reflection, negation, confirmation?
Sage welcomes all as God's almighty will
He accepts 'what is', as gracious grist to his mill.
Gently by grace of God, in mercy, he breaks all bondage bonds
In a great paean of praise and total affirmation
He rests with consciousness, his Self, the great consummation.

I have lost the monotonous merry-go-round of thought
The perpetual treadmill of self-opinion and words,
Mainly cynicism and lies, the parroting chirp of birds,
A poisonous brew so bitterly fraught
With the mistaken idea that I ought
To cherish the mind as chief.
Am I to be mugged by thought, the villainous thief?
So that is the lesson my dear Master brought,
Ignore the scorpion stings of concepts wrought
With this inner discussion and debate. It's so absurd
There is consciousness here, a gift beyond any belief
And the ending of thought; peace, ultimate joy and relief.

I am clarity pure as diamond, crystal, lily-white
Growing in a moorland, a purple thistle-bracken field.
So what is illusion? To this question I meekly yield.
Finite mind can't understand the infinite,
And magic of Maya is but a slick trick of light.
What is this life? A bad dream which appears?
A note to deceive the soundest of ears,
An emptiness as velvet void as night
For witnessing Self, nakedness of clear inward sight.
To know what is here now beyond pearl onion peeled.
So my Master gently wipes away all my sad grief and tears,
All is well, unfolding as it should to allay foolish fears.

With not the slightest hint of duality, One without two,

Unity, wholeness, existence, holistic, all seamless
Without separation, pure consciousness, love, awareness,
No division between me and you
Emanating from the Primal Source, who
Am I, but That? I am eternal, the same
Being as truth and God without a name.
At last I know the little 'me' who can never do,
All that happens is the will of God right through.
I rest in the spiritual heart, blissful, benign and blameless,
So what is my greater Self to the mighty God of flame?
My Master says "Unknown, unique, celebrate His game.

"For endless striving and effort, what's the urgent need?
Struggling, wrestling against one's natural way and feeling
Trained from the cradle to do well, and practice honest dealing,
Working hard if you wish to barely feed
A family own home, car and succeed,
Ingrained, conditioned, a machine well oiled,
Pilgrim's become half-baked and par-boiled".
So my Master to his students does plead,
Be still, motiveless when you perform any deed.
So forget all those books, aims, efforts, teaching and kneeling,
After all the hard years you've zealously worked and toiled
Open wide, relax, and never by the world be coiled!

I have no limits or borders, I am no longer bound.
No more hedges, fences, verges, remain for spacious me,
Nothing arises, I am empty capacity for all to see
That all is well, my True Self I have found!
I traced my 'I thought' like a hunting hound
And knew my primal source, the light of day,
And now as consciousness I'm free to play.
I rest in the heart on a sacred mound
Where my naked feet walk on holy ground.

I am freedom, enlightenment, joy, bliss and liberty!
Nothing ever was, I am God, what more is left to say?
This Ashtavakra taught me, his devoted pupil, the true Advaita
way!

I am That, absolute, unique, ever primeval One
As consciousness, love, awareness, effortless bliss,
Embraced by the love of God, blest by His all-gracious kiss ;
In light of glory, radiant as the sun,
I am homogeneous, second to none.
What care I for freedom or liberation?
In life or death, gaining realisation?
Or for my destiny predisposed to run,
Reborn in another womb till kingdom come?
And after transmigration, at-one-ment I may miss.
My Master halts this baffling mental perturbation.
I let go, abiding in my heart of silent adoration.

DEVOTION

The Self is very dear to all: from dearest love,
Unbroken Bhakti flows, like stream of golden oil.
Guru knows Self within, as his dear God above.
His child, after determined and persistent toil,

May see his Guru apart from Self, yet melts
Mind's strained logic, to find Faith in Him alone.
That blessed ever flowing fire of love, smelts
Soul's dross. His heart's desire, becomes his own.

The one who attaches mere form to Holy Name,
With Bhakti ripe, and knowing Truth complete,
In time transcends that image just the same.
The blossom on the bough flowers Self replete!

The fool who prays for selfish ends desired,
Fulfilment never finds; then he soon begins,
To love for sake of happiness, by God inspired.
This prayer, being granted, he conquers and wins.

In love with that One, the golden flow unceasing,
Soul grows a white lotus of purest devotion,
In calm stillness, its root in depth increasing,
Within heart's vessel to lead us o'er the ocean

Of strife, letting soul unfold, as Self of sky,
The One all wise, unlidded, and all seeing Eye!

BEWARE

Egotistic mind boasts peacock's pride,
Strutting and cavorting with arrogant stride,
It shows off its plumes for all to see,
This marvellous person that he calls me.

It goes striding through at a plod,
But rarely does it ever think of God,
Always pleasure seeking in every way,
It wastes this life in pointless play.

All such vanity leads to insanity,
Egotism is the first step to inanity,
If we wish instead to be truly wise,
Then consult Sages and their works surmise.

Ego's the path of disaster, dear friends,
For peacockism leads to fatal ends.
Be self effacing and Realise the Self,
Rather than prey to the play of that demon elf

UNSEEN WEAVER

Here stands a giant loom of Time in duration,
It is born of Infinity from a whole consummation
With Life, which has ever been void of time.
The sun and moon as shuttle upward climb
By playing, weaving to and fro as night and day,
A splendid pageant of coloured display.
All strung on warp and weft of cosmic unity,
The back of this vast embroidered tapestry
Is monochrome, derived from the formless One.
The face is multihued and radiant as Sun,
Its tones reflected from archetypal light
Unabsorbed, are an unequalled sight.
Only what's permitted by unseen hand
Appears as moving panorama, a horizontal band,
A magic painting of the whole wide world.
Brushed as vertical, each single thread is whirled
Without dimmest dint of dull duality
As Light, unique unto its Self. Sheer Reality!
Coated by golden fleece and white angelic wool,
It is dyed in deepest vat, destiny's darkened pool.
So does the holy cloth that's woven in Love
Quarrel with his weaver who rules from above?
Rather, wrapped in warmest cloak at rainbows end
Eternal pilgrim e'er adores his Mighty Friend.

SPORT

He is out today.
every bird is singing his name
every tendril towards him yearns,
each drop of morning dew
reflects the ocean of his grandeur.

The curtain of blue has lifted
to reveal a glory of Sun resplendent.
Sometimes behind a gloomy cloud
He hides in mischief sulking,
but having glimpsed in undergrowth
the hem of his robe, I know
that he is somewhere about
and enjoying the play.

Look who just flew into the room
in food-moth form!
searching for a flame
in which to be consumed.

Sometimes you wrap
Yourself in a cloak of pain
to chisel away at my basalt rock
an image of thy Name
and other days you send
a cup of nectar
for my honeybee soul to humbly sip.

DAWN

Tinted like a Tangerine, the dawn,
Amid all God's lights, the fairest sight;
Child of that prime primeval light,
The Absolute from which All is born.

Jet night, dispatched by Sun's uprising,
Has yielded up her birthplace to the morn,
Garbed in glory, golden robes, he's worn,
To herald new day's hope; oft surprising!

Expanding light soon disperses gloom,
In the shade of mind's false glimmer;
Red stains in the sky gently wane, much dimmer;
The Sun of clear vision dispels dark doom.

Our Sun's a baby star on Galaxy's edge,
But an inward Sun glows in every heart;
Man lives by this flame 'till death do us part.
Then, new dawn springs from soul's Self Knowledge.

PRANAYAMA

I open the wicket gate and walk
Onto the daisy pranked meadow,
Breathe fresh champagne air
Wafting down from green hills
Over perfumed pine forests.
I am here now,
I breathe in and out,
A whole world is created
On my transparent screen.
Thoughts fly, spiral, chirp,
Like a whirling flock of finches,
Feelings flicker and quiver
Secreting springs of joy.

My feet feel the soft grass
I bathe in its emerald sea,
I look up and see suspended,
A cloud contoured as a human-face,
An enigmatic mirror image
Asking 'who am I?

Sunbeams break through the grey sky
Catching the swarming may flies
Dancing like agitated galaxies.
I breathe in
Deep into the depths of my lungs,
Close my eyes,
This world is destroyed.

THE BOAT OF MY BEING

One evening a crescent Moon appeared,
Descended from the night and gazed at me.
As a falcon catches prey at hunting time,
This Moon snatched me up, orbiting the sky.
When I looked attentively, inside myself,
There was nobody there for me to see,
Because in that Moon's deep gaze my restless mind,
Through God's grace, was taken to my heart
And all Divine secrets, stood revealed.
The spheres of heaven merged in that bright light,
The boat of my Being sailed serenely in that sea,
Its waters became ruffled by mental waves
And the voice of Wisdom was gently heard.
Then the sea foamed, and at every fleck,
Figures formed and frothily flooded forth.
Each received a signal from within this sea
And dissolved as Spirit into that vast ocean.
Without the great power of Almighty God
One would never see the moon nor be the sea.

THY WILL BE DONE

Our hymn is sung to the Great and Wondrous One
Who dwells in splendour, a dazzling radiant light
That shines in every Heart and each manifest Sun
Of Self-effulgent beauty, blazing bright.
Thou art All, and Thy mighty will be done,
Oh make our actions worthy, in Thy holy sight.
Oh Lord, we pray to keep Thee ever in our sight,

Oh Thou whom we adore, our God the Holy One.
Your rays of Grace and Love are ever bright
In strength and power, as the awesome crimson Sun.
Oh keep us from all wavering, fix our Heart on light,
Thou art All, and Thy mighty will be done.
Thou art All, and Thy mighty will be done,

Not foolish will of ego, lest it darkens sight
And screens us from the bliss of Thee, oh Kingly One.
Thy blinding brilliance of eternity bright
Is stronger, deeper than the summer mid-day Sun.
Let us bathe in blissful balm of blessed light.
Oh lead us Lord, from nescient dark to conscious light!

Thou art All and thy mighty will be done
And ever mindful we are resting in Thy sight
For thou art Father, Mother, Teacher, Friend; oh Holy One
Your perennial fire is flaming clear and bright
Deep in the heart, a resplendent inward Sun.
He who within us hides and bides is also in the Sun,

Black clouds dispelled by beckoning beacon light.
On bended knee we glorify Thee, oh Primordial One

Who through Grace revealed demists this frosted sight.
Thou art All, and Thy mighty will be done
Polish the mirror of our Souls and make them ever bright.
Oh Jewel of Faith that ever sparkles diamond bright

And shines fiercely as our bosom friend, the Sun,
Thaw the frigid heart with warmth and light
Thou art All and thy mighty will be done.
Oh let our acts be worthy, in Thy holy sight,
A hymn to be sung to the Great and Wondrous One.
Praise to the Holy One, ever burning beryl bright,

May His wisdom light guide us as the Sun
And may His will be done, in His all loving sight.

WORLD ILLUSION

Ego's driven by crude desires for pleasure,
Pleasures without graded gauge or measure,
It views sex, riches, and goods as treasure;
Unrestrained, it races after aimless leisure.

'Twould be wiser to be much more profound,
Reflect on wisdom the Great Sages found;
Control mind, bury ego deep in the ground,
Build one's shrine of Liberation on its mound.

Let life glow golden, not grimly greyer,
That must be our fervent earnest prayer;
Surrender to God's will as a brave yea-sayer,
Love one's own dear Self as one's near neighbour.

Great Ramana, save me from world delusion,
I'm suffering from ego's grave illusion,
Mundane mind's sunk in constant confusion,
Grant me Thy gaze, such divinest diffusion.

To be freed from Jagat Maya is our goal,
Self Realisation's the means to make one whole,
A pure, consciously aware liberated soul;
For men and women, our true birth rights' role!

WHAT AM I?

Am I a piano virtuoso of words,
Tinkling verbs, adjectives and nouns for all I'm worth,
Strumming a sonata of nonsensical sound?
Or is there in me a nest of pretty parrot birds,
Squawking day and night ever since my awkward birth?
But there's a secret to end this disease I've found.

All that's mischievous monkey mind my fine friend,
It clouds the shining Sun of Self, my Real Being,
By diving into the Heart with all of my might,
I slay mad egotism and pronounce its timely end,
Questioning where's its source? I give it a fright,
Then arises the bliss of freedom and Self Revealing!

JOY RIDE

Joyous jubilation is the jester's song,
Sweet tonic to right all doleful wrong.
From the heart it rings a happy chime,
And rescues mind from dull despondent time.

So roar from the roof tops with all ones might,
God's shines from His heaven and all is right!
Bury mad melancholy in a deep black hole,
And much sooner we'll save our wretched soul.

Laughter makes us loose our worry and care,
So unbutton our coats and let down our hair!
The world's not a place for shame or for woe,
That's the quick route to hell that we know.

'Row row row the boat gently down the stream,
Merrily, merrily for life is but a dream'!
So the message for each golden girl and boy,
Is find true love and laughter, in warm hearts of joy'!

DEEP HEART DIVING

If constant, persistent deep heart diving
Is consistent, and truly thriving,
Ego has no more hope of ever surviving.

Nerves continually turning and churning,
Vasanas on fire and briskly burning;
The Jiva prays, desperately yearning.

Such is deft deep diving within, to reach
The root of ego, my Guru does teach,
A way of Self Enquiry for one and each.

With strong energetic plunge and lusty surge,
Malign tendencies we purge and then emerge;
Again we dive within when there's the urge.

Our aim's to find the precious lustrous pearl,
Of Self's brilliant splendour. 'Twill unfurl,
Let Sat-Chit-Ananda curl, in wondrous whirl.

The sacred task is to waken soul from sleep,
For that, dive in the Heart's a quantum leap,
The way to Liberation, evermore to keep.

WELCOME

Greeted by fiery splendour of the golden dawn,
A bright new day begins, each fine auspicious morn.

We welcome all that happens, both inside and out,
For all's His Grace without a hint of doubt.

What ever God sends us, is always for the best,
As children on His path we're very, very blest.

All are predestined to perform His mighty will,
Whether one likes it or not for good or for ill.

He knows what's most needed to heal each soul,
To wake and shake us up, and so make us whole.

With Faith, we hand him all our worldly cares,
Such trust's a quantum leap for the one who dares.

We free the mind from foolish thoughts that run to fear,
And save errant soul from drowning in sadness drear.

Vain ego says 'I'm the doer, the one who knows',
But the Lord makes us see by shocks and blows,

All is for our good, to make us search within,
And end all sad sinful woes, and freedom win!

PARAMOUNT DUTY

There's a vast ocean of bluish green beauty,
Reminding us it's our paramount duty,
To plunge into the Heart, and seek the source
Of foul ego with all our might and force.

That ocean's the symbol of the spiritual heart,
Which we must probe until one day that part
Of vile vasanas departs the monkey mind,
And then Enlightenment is there we find.

So suggested beloved Sage Ramana,
The Blessed Lord of Mount Arunachala.
He brought Atma Vichara right to the fore,
To help suffering devotees for ever more,
And save them from dreaded dire samsara.
Such was the greatness of dear Sage Ramana!

APPEARANCE AND REALITY

People viewed are phantoms in a dream,
Puppets held in the gloved hand of God,
On a screen of consciousness, Self throws a gleam;
All's evolved somehow, it's so strange and odd.

The garden hedge of Advaita is sewn,
With rose bushes of potent paradox,
Foxing monkey mind; how high they've grown.
Truth is neither orthodox nor heterodox.

What's called Truth, empirically forsooth,
Is false metaphysically it seems,
And vice versa, that's the huge joke of Truth,
In this perplexed vexed maze of sunbeams.

We stop posing problems with the brain,
But practise Self Enquiry and Surrender,
That's all that's needed on this train;
Mental rubbish, best we trash in a blender.

The egotistic mind is mostly mad,
Just a muddled mix of mundane thought,
Neither very good nor very bad,
Ever telling us what we 'should' and 'ought'.

'So what we see is not what it seems or appears',
So the Great Advaita Sages wisely state,
We strive to see who's the see-er and who hears?
And never leave the Task before 'tis much too late!

TRUTH

Multiformed, multibrained, pilgrim man,
Intent on a mission daring and brave,
'Twas his wholehearted devoted plan
To discover God's Truth and himself save..

Somewhat bemused, puzzled and vexed,
He laboured with books to search and to scan,
To learn pure wisdom and help perplexed
Tormented soul, in the best way he can.

After much reading and seeking for truth,
He came upon the teaching of one great Sage,
Overjoyed in this high moment forsooth,
He came to Ramana, blessing for our Age.

The Jnani focused his forceful gaze
On pilgrim, making contact eye to eye,
His power of consciousness like a blaze,
Evoked the Self, a Truth he could not deny.

He told him "Surrender and enquire my son,
That's my direct path to Realisation,
Strive with brave persistence until you've won
Moksha- the goal for man, soul's consummation! "

Pilgrim struggled with grave might and main,
But became discouraged unable to trace
The source of his ego; was all in vain?
'Til there descended the great power of Grace.

'Twas if he'd been given Love's kindest kiss,

He felt sheer existence and awareness pure,
The full Realised Self was infinite bliss,
For his prisoned soul, the absolute cure!

END OF SEEKING

It's over now my end of seeking
Now's the time, I surrender to 'THE All'.

Behind the veil my Self is peeking,
Obey my Voice! I answer His urgent call.

"Dive within the Heart dear earnest friend,
And samsara's bad dream you now shall end!"

The buds will open on the almond tree,
Some come first, they yearn to be free.

Some come later but in His good time
All will abide in the Lord Divine.

Souls need Self's bright sun of Guru's Grace,
Nowhere God is not, ever there in place.

LOVE*

Love's way is humility and intoxication,
The torrent floods down. How can it run up?
You'll be a cabochon in the ring of lovers,
If you're a red ruby's slave, dear friend ;
Even as Earth is a serf of sapphire sky
And your monkey body's a slave to your spirit.

What did Earth ever lose by this relationship?
What mercy has the Self showed to weary limbs?
One shouldn't beat the snare drum of awakening
Beneath a cosy sofa's, comfy counterpane.

Hoist, like a hero, your flag in the desert.
Listen with your soul's ear to the song,
In that hollow of the vast turquoise dome,
Rising from the lover's passionate moan

When your tight gown-strings are loosened
By the tipsy inebriation of perfect love,
The victorious heavens shout, triumphantly!
And the constellations gaze down ashamed.

This world is in deep trouble, from top to bottom,
But it can be swiftly healed by the balm of love.

*A versification from Rumi's Divan based on the Nicholson
Literal Translation

NATARAJAN

Grand symphony of life, music of the spheres,
Unfolds like Shiva's dance, stamping on my breast;
Aware, one feels a martial drumming beat, and hears
Joyful rhythm that cheers the heart, and I am blest.

His footprints leave a lesson on my book of time,
They make a mark on my inconscient wall,
To learn from, so that soul may swiftly climb,
To conquer life's mysterious enigmatic All.

I ascend on eagle's wings into the great unknown,
Lord Shiva steers my flight through bliss and pain,
In this paradoxical way I'm stretched and grown,
Yet his merciful bliss soon soothes my nervous pain.

Let's give thanks and praise for Lord Shiva's cosmic dance,
Grounding arrogant ego into chalky powdered dust,
It's predetermined, nothing is left to random chance,
It's choreographed, infinitely wise, precise and just.

MUCH ADO ABOUT NOTHING

"There's no Time; it's a mode of convenience, thought up by Man,

No Space ,a Theatrical Stage set up by our pre-programmed brain,

No body ,just molecules, atoms, that revolve in Self's own span,

No mind, a narrow gauge to measure things, on our Dreamer's Train,

No Good nor Evil, Right nor Wrong, these are polarities of the Age,

Nothing perceived or conceived is "Real",so says the Advaita Vedantic Sage.

SAGE WISDOM*

Whoever is awake to the material world
Is fast asleep to the spiritual world.
This wakefulness is far worse than sleep,
When our soul's asleep to God, it's a door
Closing, to prevent the entry of His grace.
All day we suffer from a host of fantasies,
Thoughts of loss, gain or degeneration.
For the Soul there is neither joy nor peace
Nor a way of progression heavenwards.
The sleeper has his hope in each vain fancy
And converses idly with these foolish voices.

The bird of the soul flies cheerily on high
While its shadow is speeding upon Earth,
Some fools hasten to chase their shadow
And rushing hurriedly become exhausted,
Not understanding that it's a reflection,
Nor knowing from where it originates.

They vainly shoot arrows at this phantom,
His quiver soon empties from the long quest.
The contents of his worried life become a void,
Time passes in chasing after this grey shadow.
But when God's shadow becomes a nurse maid.
It saves him from fantasies and illusion.
God's shadow is the true servant of God.

Dead to this world yet living through Him.
Take hold of His hem quickly so your skirt
May also be saved at the end of your days.
Never enter this dark valley of the shadow

Without a guide who's a true son of God.
Desert the grey shadow, gain the bright Sun
Hold the hem of the orb of Shams Tabriz.

If you don't know the way to the bridal feast
Enquire into God's radiance named El'Haqq.
If envy grabs you by the throat on the way
It is Satan who reaches beyond all bounds.
Because from green envy he hates Adam
And he's at constant war with happiness.

On the way there's no harder bridge to cross.
Happy is he who hasn't made envy his friend.
The body is a mansion packed full of hate,
The family and servants are all tainted.
Yet Almighty God made the body to be pure
So sweep clean His house. The purified heart
Is a true treasure and Earth's gold talisman.

If you indulge in guile, deceit and envy
Against one who's without a hint of blame,
Then black stains swell up in your heart.
So rest as dust under the feet of a Sage
Amd scatter the dust on envy's bald head.

Any fool who torments his body is unfit
For comprehending the spiritual life .
The nose catches fragrance leading to truth
That scent is the God revealed religion.
If he's whiffed this perfume with ingratitude,
It comes and destroys his organ of perception.

Give thanks! Be a slave to those who are grateful,
Be in their presence as one truly steadfast.

*A versification from Rumi's Mathnawi
The Complete Literal Translation by Reynard Nicholson

SELF ENQUIRY

Hear this, comprehend clearly as transparent air!
I'm not what I think or imagine that I am;
I'm aware like a cat stalking his fare, I'm aware
I'm not this body, earthy pot of red blooded jam,
Nor mind, mere mechanical word secreting machine,
Or a 'me' who peeps from behind a measly mince meat ball,
A dreamer, deluded by pics which flick across my screen
Of Consciousness, an empty space for 'what is' to fall,
So I leave this torrid, troubled toxic world alone.

Where is the rightful place in 'who I really am?'
An illusive surface, a shimmer, why mourn or moan
About this sandy desert with its camel caravan?
Drug induced visions like Kubla Khan or Avalone,
Emanate from mind, like mists, when hot breath hits cold air.
There's no time, a clockwork convenience conceived by man,
Space and causality are concepts in the errant brain,
No substance, but atoms dancing in an aeon's span,
No mind, a measuring tape, used on this dreamer's train.

No good or evil, right or wrong, fashions of an Age,
Only a birds nest of thoughts, it's best left to lose.
"Nothing perceived or conceived is Real" says my Sage,
"You're not what you seem to be and no one to choose.
So called choice is illusion in the predestined plan,
Free will's only apparent, and ego's pride we use
To usurp Divine Will as mine; that's the sin of Man.
There's nothing, in Truth, for anyone to will or decide,
Know 'That', and be happy, end all thoughts of suicide.

I am eternal, as Consciousness, I am 'That',

Beyond concepts of Holy Father or Mother's balm.
Truth is heard by those who at the feet of Sages sat.
Remember the verse in King David's favoured psalm,
'Be still and know that I Am God' stay silent and calm.
Words are erudite, the real point they always miss,
The Holy Aim is beyond comprehension, I repeat,
The veil that conceals the source of speech is remiss
The other side of knowing is silence, peace replete.

When in mind, I think this world isn't a dream but real,
I feel separate from my Source, yet know all is well,
Unfolding precisely as it must; I trust and feel
No need to bargain with God, as far as I can tell,
All's well each moment, I know 'That' so I let all heal.
Nothing exists, not even these thoughts, they're a thorn
To remove thorns; in Truth there is no thing at all.
I rest, desiring nothing, I am thus unborn,
Empty to be Pure Self Awareness, for peace may fall.

My reason has been jolted, shaken to its inmost core,
By my wildly strange adventures, uniquely so bizarre;
Who am I? to be feeling there's no 'me'? shout hurrah!
I seem to be, intuition, that's flooding through the door,
Drowning my brain and sense perceptions, near and far.
Is there anyone here? Is Awareness my real identity?
Then thoughts broke in and ended my earnest Self Inquiry.
I'm moved again to play the sportive game of life,
Merrily dancing to circumstances piped by drum and fife.

BRIEF GLOSSARY

Advaita
Not Two
The Philosophy and Teaching of Non Dualism

Arunachala
The Sacred Mountain at Tiruvannamalai known to be a descent
of Lord Shiva

Ashtavakra
The famous Sage who brought King Janaka to Self Realisation

Atman
Atma Vichara
Self Enquiry
Turning the mind inward to search for the source of the ego

Agni
God of Fire
Intermediary between man and Iswara (Almighty God)
according to the Rig Veda

Ajnani
A Soul still steeped in ignorance

Ananda
Bliss

Aum
The sacred primeval universal sound. The Word.

Bhagavan
Godlike

Bhakti
The Path of Devotion

Brahma
The Creator God in the Hindu Pantheon

Brahman
The Supreme Absolute

Eki Sloka
A key verse epitomising a Sage's Teaching

Ganapati
The Elephant God who removes obstacles

Ganglion Knot
The Granthi- a link formed between the mind and the Self which has to be severed for Self Realisation to take place

Hanuman
The powerful Monkey God who assisted Lord Rama

Hara
An epithet of Shiva

Jai
Victory

Jiva
Soul

Jnana
Self Knowledge

Jnani
The Enlightened Sage

Kavakanti
Great Poet

Maharshi
Great Rishi

Maha Deva
Great God

Manmatha
A Demon

Maya
Illusion

Moksha
Enlightenment

Nirvana
Absolute freedom

Om
The same as AUM

Om Namah Bhagavate Sri Ramanayah
The mantra for Ramana Maharshi

Parvati
Consort of Lord Shiva

Pranayama
The Yogic Science of Breathing

Puja
Religious ceremony

Rama
Hero of the Ramanaya. An incarnation of Vishnu

Ramana
Ramana maharshi

Sadhana
Spiritual Practice

Sadhak
Pilgrim

Sambhu
An affectionate name for Lord Shiva

Samsara
The repetitive cycle of birth and rebirth

Shankara
Adi Shankara- the great consolidator of the Advaita Teaching

Shiva
The God of Creation , Maintenance and Disolution

Skanda
Warrior son of Shiva

Sat Chit Ananda
Reality-Consciousness-Bliss

Sat Guru
Inner Guru

Taraka
Demon likened to Egotism

Uma
Affectionate name of Parvati

Vasanas
Latent Tendencies which form the unconscious

Vishnu
God as Universal Sustainer

Yama
God of Death

AUTHOR'S BIOGRAPHY

Alan Jacobs is President of the Ramana Maharshi Foundation UK and has made a life long study of Comparative Religion and Mysticism.As a Poet he studied at Morley College under Christopher Reid and at the City Literary Institute under Julia Casterton. He has studied extensively the works of Sri Bhagavan Ramana Maharshi, Adi Shankara, Arthur Schopenhauer, George Gurdjieff, and J.Krishnamurti. He has mainly lived in London. He attended Malvern College , Worcester, and was A Business Man , Art Dealer, and Professional Life Coach before turning to Authorship. As a Poet he has authored two collections and is published regularly in the Poetry Magazine Reflections , occasionally in the Magazine, The Mountain Path and on the www. Advaita Academy. His Poetry Blog is at alanjacobs.blogspot.com He has a Profesional Page on Face Book: Alan Jacobs Poet Writer Author

His published books include 17th C Dutch and Flemish Painters, A Collectors Guide, The Gnostic Gospels, The Essential Gnostic Gospels, The Bhagavad Gita, The Principal Upanishads, The Spiritual Meditations of Marcus Aurelius, all of which are Poetic Transcreations. He has authored When Jesus Lived in India, a Modernized Abridgement of Plato's Republic, Ramana Maharshi Supreme Guru, and edited Ramana Shankara and the Forty Verses. His Novellas are Eutopia and Socrates Without Tears .He has compiled the Anthologies, Reflections, Native American Wisdom, Poetry For the Spirit, Peace of Mind, The Ocean of Wisdom, The Wisdom of Balsekar, the Dalai lama, Mahatma Gandhi and Henry David Thoreau . His own Poetry Collections are Mastering Music Walks The Sun-Lit Sea and Myrobalan of the Magi.

Born in 1929, he lives in London, has three children and six grand children. He visits India annually.

Index of first lines

BOOKS

O is a symbol of the world, of oneness and unity. In different cultures it also means the "eye," symbolizing knowledge and insight. We aim to publish books that are accessible, constructive and that challenge accepted opinion, both that of academia and the "moral majority."

Our books are available in all good English language bookstores worldwide. If you don't see the book on the shelves ask the bookstore to order it for you, quoting the ISBN number and title. Alternatively you can order online (all major online retail sites carry our titles) or contact the distributor in the relevant country, listed on the copyright page.

See our website **www.o-books.net** for a full list of over 500 titles, growing by 100 a year.

And tune in to myspiritradio.com for our book review radio show, hosted by June-Elleni Laine, where you can listen to the authors discussing their books.

MySpiritRadio